THE

9

TENETS OF A SUCCESSFUL RELATIONSHIP

by Jay Hurt

PENDIUM

PUBLISHING HOUSE
514-201 Daniels Street
Raleigh, NC 27605

For information, please visit our Web site at
www.pendiumpublishing.com

PENDIUM Publishing and its logo
are registered trademarks.

The 9 Tenets of a Successful Relationship
BY Jay Hurt

Copyright © Jay Hurt, 2011
All Rights Reserved.

ISBN: **978-1-936513-08-6**

PUBLISHER'S NOTE

TABLE of CONTENTS

- The Foundation (Chapters 1-3)

We must make good choices as a starting point. This chapter focuses on decision making.

Let's expound on the process around making thorough decisions. "If it don't fit, don't force it. Just relax and let it go."

To know what we want, we must truly know ourselves. Knowing your self-worth, your value to others and who you truly are is a prerequisite of being a part of any successful relationship.

- The Infrastructure (Chapters 4-12) THE *9 TENETS*

***TENET #1 Work on Your Relationship Constantly for it to Thrive**
You will have to make a concerted effort to have a successful relationship. This chapter will touch on ways to work on your relationship on a consistent basis.

***TENET #2 Communicate Clearly and Effectively**
Understanding how we communicate with each other is crucial. We will address how to hear each other as well as how to talk to each other in this chapter.

***TENET #3 Listen to Your Own Advice**
Often we let our emotional attachment override the common sense we were blessed with. We will discuss using discernment to separate the feeling of being needed as opposed to the feeling of truly being loved and appreciated. We know these things innately when we share our opinions with others. We will discuss applying it to our own situations.

***TENET #4 Do Not Live with Someone Before Marriage**
Cohabitation is often a precursor to disaster in relationships. We will explore the benefits and detriments of living together without true commitment in covenant.

***TENET #5 Show Appreciation**
We will experience what it looks like to make the extra effort to show how much we appreciate each other.

***TENET #6 Decide if You Can Live with the Flaws**
No one is perfect, no matter how beautiful, charming, intelligent or classy they are. This chapter will touch on imperfection and how to deal with it.

***TENET #7 Continue to Date Throughout the Relationship**
Discussion about how to avoid developing a routine which entails taking each other for granted.

***TENET #8 Concentrate on Growing Together**
This chapter will speak to how developing a path to your dreams and aspirations is vital to the success of your relationship.

***TENET #9 Love, Honor and Respect**
The essence of a successful relationship is explored in this chapter. Loving someone in every way, honoring them as though you are in covenant and respecting that person the same as you expect to receive respect is synonymous with success.

- The Accessories (Chapters 13-15)

This chapter takes an in-depth look at sexuality in today's pre-marital culture. We will discuss misconceptions and exploits in our society which often make our sexuality contribute to the problems of our relationships as opposed to being the blessing it was designed to be.

Romance without finance has no chance...or does it? A chapter dedicated to sharpening our skills on working together to alleviate the financial challenges of building a relationship.

We are merging more and more children into families in the present time. We will take a look at how to understand from the point we decide to unite, we have to become accepting and appreciative of the new children in our families.

- The Culmination (Chapter 16)

This chapter will take a moment of reflection on the lessons we have discussed. The culmination of the journey of the book signals the opportunity to bring a new beginning to your relationship.

Acknowledgments

There are many people who contributed to this writing. Some knowingly, and probably some that never will. I am sure those most important in my life will be well aware of their contributions. I will never be able to give everyone who contributed to this book my personal heartfelt thanks. If I leave someone out of verbal appreciation or otherwise, please charge it to my head and not my heart as I sincerely love and appreciate each and every person who has been a part of this journey.

First and foremost, nothing in my life is complete without my Lord and Savior, Jesus. I appreciate the gift He gave to us, and I am constantly awed by the way He allows me to have a successful relationship with Him, once I chose eternal life over certain death. May He continue to bless us all, and may I be blessed with humility, wisdom, and most of all, a heart that yearns for His Spirit to dwell in me. He will make the crooked places straight, and I am a living testimony to those words.

My appreciation goes out to my two motivating factors, my daughters, Kristina and Jalen. Without them, there is no drive, no determination, no perseverance, no book. My prayer is they grow to understand we can do all things through Christ and there is nothing they cannot achieve. My two, beautiful charismatic daughters will impact the world someday, and I am thankful and humbled to be their father. I love you both more than you can ever imagine. Daddy

I love you, Mom and my niece Jaesha and my nephew Jaydon. You guys are my motivation as well. My biggest fan probably doesn't know that I'm her biggest fan, my strong, supportive and beautiful sister Sherricka, Love you sis!

I want to thank the ladies and gentlemen represented in this book. Although we quickly find it's not really about the characters in the story, it's more about the character of the story, I appreciate you sharing with me the things you went through to grow and develop. It's normally not easy to share with someone, and probably least of all to share with me since I can be a bit harsh at time. Please understand my characteristic stern approach is always tempered with love as I want the best for those who are close to me, and for those who simply share with me.

I would be remiss to leave out those who helped me with the contents of *9 Tenets*. A sincere "thank you" goes out to Robert Zaloba. I asked for your expertise and for you not to hold back, and I must say, you definitely didn't hold back! Your wisdom and guidance has given me the opportunity to develop my thoughts in a way which turned my compilation of thoughts into a book and for that I am grateful. To my other editors, that worked with me throughout this process: I don't know that I have permission to put their names here, so I will say that I love you both, and there is definitely no way this ever gets off the ground without either of you. I would like to tell you both that I am forever in your debt, but knowing you as well as I do, I'm sure I will be paying up as soon as possible!

I would like to thank Pendium Publishing for having the confidence in me to publish my book. I want to thank my friend, Shellie, for putting me on to them.

I have the best friends in the world. Jody and Kenny, I appreciate you having my back as I was working through this project. Troy, you wrote a book while I was writing this one—how ironic! I hope it's a best seller. Jonathan, I appreciate you holding me down from the other side of the country. Laura and Sherri, I can't leave the two lovely ladies out who talk me through my challenges and force me to think outside the box. Love both of yall! Christi, you are always holding me down as well, love you too!

Finally, thanks to everyone for giving me support and courage to undertake something of this magnitude. To those who were there for me, I remain in your debt and I am always grateful for your presence in my life and in this book. My prayer is someone applies the knowledge given in this book, and then gives the glory and honor to the Lord as He is our provider for all things—including successful relationships!

INTRODUCTION

First of all, I would like to say I am writing this book to assist people like those I know in my inner circle, people everywhere who have had challenging relationships and not to mention, myself. I have found we all want many of the same things. We want to have relationships which thrive and where the couple grows together. It seems the challenge is, there are so many factors which play a part in learning what thriving is and what simply surviving is. We also have many things to consider which our parents and grandparents did not have, when building lives for themselves. For example, many of us are combining families. There are a lot of single parents out there who are bringing children which they have raised a certain way and the other party is bringing a child (or children) which they have raised a different way and now they have to work to find a common ground. Some believe in corporal punishment, others do not. Some believe their children should have a better life as children than they did, while others believe that not giving the kids a lot and making them earn just as they did is the right way to rear a child. Then, we have so many cultures and backgrounds to consider as we decide to engage in relationships. There are many religions to consider, so that brings another challenge to the table…"I love you…but you are a (denomination X) and I was not raised that way." All of these things are relatively new challenges we have to overcome as we establish relationships.

Within the last decade, the world has grown into one universal economy and job market. This gives us an entirely new plethora of issues. Employers sometimes want us to move around the country and sometimes around the world to move up the corporate ladder. We are uprooting families to follow careers, chase dreams and paychecks. All of these things are to say the least, an inconvenience, in building relationships and lives with people we care about. We need to consider all of these things when choosing a mate. This reality is sometimes eased (and burdened) by the advent of long distance relationships. We can so easily touch one another with cell phones, texting, IM, Twitter, MySpace, Facebook and other methods of communication; we are often choosing to extend the relationship possibilities outside of our city, state, or even our country! Many will say no one is farther than a six-hour plane ride from anyone anywhere in the continental United States. Though that fact may be true, I think we are losing the personal touch we need to have to make relationships strong, make them work and last. As I delve into the nine tenets which help to build a successful relationship (starting in Chapter Four), I will work on the art of making our relationships more interpersonal, more intimate and more fulfilling overall.

I am extremely blessed to have people around me who believe in me. They appreciate my advice and share their experiences with me. Everything I will teach in this book is a compilation of what I have learned as I have studied my friends, family and every part of the environment around me. The experiences I share will be derived from situations I have seen, heard, or been a part of, or a compilation of those situations. College taught me many great things, but life has taught me one thing that college could not teach me: A lot of things sound great in theory, but often there are many different results when put into application. Simplified, some things make sense, but in the reality of our world in the 21st century, sometimes what makes sense is not easily accomplished. This is often the case especially when our hearts, our emotions, our money and our love are all a part of the equation. I want to make these situations easier, not only for my friends, but for you (and for me for that matter). I write this book out of love for my friends. I want to share the common denominators which can make the relationships for them and for you better, going forward.

We will touch on many relationship issues, most often from the single perspective. The reality is relationship challenges are all around us. Some of the most common issues we probably all have dealt with at some point are basic work place relationship issues. Often we are forced to deal with someone we do not like for a variety of reasons. There are times where the relationship issue is submitting to authority, or an abusiveness of power. There may be problems with communicating with someone, often because of the cultural differences in the workplace. Everyone has opinions, values and standards they bring with them wherever they go, so they cannot be expected to agree and be in unison on every issue which may arise on a day to day basis. A manager's job in the workplace is to delegate and make sure the job gets done, but on another level, his job is to facilitate relationships. He must make sure his team is on the same page, no matter their personal differences, to work together in harmony to get things done. The co-workers do not have to hold hands and sing "Joy to the World" as they work, but the important point here is they have to have a working relationship.

Individually, we deal with relationship challenges every day on every level. One of the key relationships we have is the relationship with our friends. Personally I have friends of many ethnicities, ages, both genders and live all over the world. Technology has made it easier for us to keep in contact with each other, although we may be on different continents. Also, I have several close friends in my inner circle that I see quite often. In my individual case, the people I am closest to are quite opinionated, and interestingly enough, we often do not agree. We may not agree on minor issues like where to choose to go get a Latte, or much deeper issues such as why (or why not) we think healthcare reform is good for America. Regardless of our differences, we remain friends, in a few cases for over twenty years. My friends and I learned long ago to communicate openly and honestly and respect each other's differences. Some of my greatest memories when hanging out with my friends are debates about opinions of someone's thoughts on 'is Christ is the Messiah?' or 'who is better, Kobe or Michael?' We have differences, sometimes even in faith (a very important topic to me), but that does not keep me from respecting their opinions and often agreeing to disagree. A friendship is a relationship which also requires managing the relationship, just as a work relationship and a romantic relationship.

An interesting factor in our friendships is we feel less pressure and we do not feel we have an expectation to attain. At work, we have quotas to meet, a production schedule to hit. The pressure of the job often adds to the pressure of work relationships. Quite often, we feel less pressure in the early stages of a romantic relationship. There is some pressure: A pressure to impress so a couple can develop the relationship beyond a platonic relationship. Normally, there is a lot of euphoria as two people are getting to know one another, so the pressure is often alleviated until the relationship has some depth. As time progresses, there is not much pressure to a date with someone we have dated for a few months. There is pressure in a relationship when we have to rely on someone to pay the bills, pick up the kids, help someone take their daily medicine, etc.

The challenges of relationships (the relationship between a man and a woman) are what we will primarily deal with in this book. The infinite things we face on a daily basis are overwhelming and when we step back to think about it, almost mind-boggling. There is a reason divorce rates are higher now than when our parents were getting married. We have many things that intervene in our relationships every day. I present this as a guide to work within the reality of our lives as they are in the twenty-first century, while continuing to cultivate relationships. These relationships have been the same yesterday, today and will be the same tomorrow—only with different outside influences. I will help to navigate those influences. This book will be a blueprint on how to develop from the dating aspect of the relationship to a happy, healthy, committed, God-centered relationship. Ladies, we are going to learn to love our men and be a true help-mate in a great way. Not in the way society has turned the idea of being a help-mate into being an indentured servant, but the way God intended for a help-mate to be: a blessed contributor to the covenant. Gentlemen, we are going to learn to love our women as Christ loved the Church. The way we are supposed to, the way our Creator intended it to be.

There are not many guarantees in life. I can unequivocally say I have one guarantee for you in this book. If you will apply what I will teach here, you will see a marked improvement in your relationships. Once you read the book, pick one tenet you find to be challenging in your relationship. It does not matter if you have been married for the past twenty-five years, or if you have been dating for three months. I will make these tenets very clear, so it will quickly become recognizable which tenets are working and which tenets are not working in your relationship. If you will commit to working on just ONE of these tenets for thirty days, you will see a better relationship. You will begin to see a change almost immediately; but you have to stick to it for thirty days-we want to build this tenet to become part of "the character of your relationship." I will discuss nine tenets, but pick the one which you would like to try to better your situation. Now, imagine what will happen when you add the next tenet in the next thirty days and the third tenet in month three. Relationships are not meant to be perfect...they are a work in progress. I want to teach you how to be aware of the right things to work on and how to work on those things. This will enable you to develop a relationship the significant other who will eventually become your spouse. The building blocks of these tenets will cause you to have a life together which you will both cherish.

THE

9

TENETS OF A SUCCESSFUL
RELATIONSHIP

Chapter One
THE CHOICES WE MAKE

I want to talk about my expertise for a moment, in the subject of relationships. I am not a PhD, I do not have a degree in psychology and I have not been married for twenty-five years. If you can get past those things and you want to continue reading; you will learn valuable information which will change your life and the character of your current and future relationships. Here is some of who I am, as opposed to who I am not. I am a person who studies my environment and I learn from it. I am a sum of everything that has ever happened to me or around me. Most importantly for you, I am someone who understands what relationships are built on and what makes them last.

You will find in this book, I will draw from experiences around me which I learned from. I evaluated the information and now I am passing along the results to you. I have nine tenets which when followed, will guarantee a strong, healthy, loving relationship. Some of the tenets will deal with the beginning of the relationship. Others will make us consider reevaluating the relationship we may currently be a part of, or the relationship we may be considering. The remaining tenets will make us show how much we appreciate one another and show love for what it really is…a verb disguised as a noun.

We have many choices to make on a daily basis; what to wear, which latte to buy at Starbucks, which side of my butt can my boss can kiss, since he/she is clearly trippin', what time to go to lunch, which thing we will put off at work until tomorrow, what to eat for dinner and which reality show to watch as we wind down. So many choices…so little time.

We make choices in relationships as well. Should we go to a movie? Dinner? Dinner and a movie? Do we want to take a vacation together? Should we take the kids? Should we leave them at home? Should we get curtains or blinds? Should I clean the house before my husband gets home? Should I cook for my boo? Should I make love to him, even though he has been trippin'? Should I look at this gorgeous woman walking by, knowing it may ruin the rest of my day if my girl catches me? Decisions, decisions, decisions…

I am having a little fun with the choices I referred to, but it is true; we have a lot of decisions and choices to make over the course of a day, week, month, year and lifetime. I have seen a lot of choices around me in relationships. Some good, some great… some…well…not so much. The point is that WE have the choice. We do not have Chinese water torture making us agree to accept something that does not work for us. What I find throughout the people I have studied is one very, very, much-too-common denominator: They feel they do not have a choice. My book is for everyone, but *this* point is especially directed to the ladies. Ladies, if you don't want to be in a situation, please understand--you do not have to be. Here are some common examples of what kind of choices we have to deal with:

- Single parent homes: I know he takes care of your kids, and their own Dad will not take care of them. That does not give him a license to not fulfill you in other ways. You cannot and will not settle for less from today forward.

- "A good man is hard to find syndrome": I realize he may be the only man you feel has ever loved you, but the reason you feel this way is because you continue to settle for less. You will not step away from a "tolerable" situation and give another man an opportunity to be "fulfilling" and actually love you the way you deserve to be loved. It is great that he may say he loves you, but that is not enough. There is so much more to it than that. Starting today, we are done with making bad choices in men and I am here to tell you there is "A better man to be found." These are the types of choices you deal with constantly so now we will learn how to make better choices so you find better men.

Do not misinterpret what am I saying when I talk about him expressing his love for you. It is a good thing to express your feelings. I do not know if anyone I know says "I love you" more than I do. I tell my children I love them all the time. I have one child who I tell "I love you," and she is not very affectionate, so she will often respond with "mmm hmmm." I know she loves me and I do not force her to say it. She understands love is really an action word and she shows her love to me through her actions. She sneaks and says I love you every now and then, just because she recognizes I like to hear it and to put some icing on a new pair of sunglasses or sneakers she just received.

When this book was going through the editing process, my editor called me on something very important I always simply assumed everyone understood. My editor said that I assumed the reader understood what "love" is. He pointed out this is probably a faulty assumption with some of you. This required some thought on my part. My first thought was, "Who doesn't know what love is?" That thought when mixed with some of the stories you will read about makes it extremely clear that many of us have no idea what love is, so let's touch on it.

In its essence, our Creator is Love. He showed us how He is love in several ways. He loved us enough to make us and loved us enough to send His Son so we may be reconciled to Him, if we choose to accept Him. Although this book is about relationships, the fact of Divine Love is important to understand the true meaning and the essence of love. One really must know what love looks like to understand if they really have someone who loves them and the relationship is reciprocal or if this is something different than love. Dictionary.com's first four definitions of love as a noun are:

- a profoundly tender, passionate affection for another person.
- a feeling of warm personal attachment or deep affection, as for a parent, child, or friend.

- sexual passion or desire.

- a person toward whom love is felt; beloved person; sweet heart.

I also want to give a few of the synonyms of love from Dictionary.com. Some of those are: exalt, affection, weakness, allegiance, emotion. I wanted to point these out because I doubt many of you have ever looked up the word, but I am sure all of us know what it means, or at least what it means to us. There is no doubt, we all have our own definition of love. Let's discuss about what we see as definitions and what is missing from these definitions.

Dictionary.com hits the nail on the head. A profoundly tender, passionate affection. If you love someone, you definitely have those types of feelings for a person. Another definition is a feeling of a warm personal attachment, or deep affection. We all feel like we are attached to our significant other. There is the definition that says, a sexual passion or desire. Sex is an important component of a relationship and that desire is the component of a successful relationship. That does not mean to act on it quite yet, but in due time. We will explore that later in the book. A person toward whom love is felt; beloved, sweetheart-that is another definition. I would say that in another way. I would say, "A person who I would sacrifice for, a person for whom I would make changes. A person for who my love is so intense, I would lay down my life for." Love, in its essence, is very serious. It is not to be taken lightly. A mother who loves her child will gladly trade her life for his, if it meant he could live. A spouse or family member will give an organ or blood transfusion to someone they love. People do not give body parts as some act of meeting some random quota on kindness. They do this out of love.

I wanted to dramatize love, because I know we often dramatize everything around the love itself. We live our lives out in what we think are romantic tragedies. Romeo and Juliet is the most popular example of a romantic tragedy. The real life tragedies these days are not so much forbidden love, as they are the fact we are confused about what love is, so the stories have a tragic ending (or at least life-altering). Juliet was not upset because Romeo was chasing other women, or Romeo was being abusive to her. Juliet was not upset with Romeo because he was trying to run back to his "baby's mama" (I hate that term, but you get the point).

Love by definition is not abusive. It is not condescending. Love is not selfish. Love is not disrespectful. Love is not insulting. Love is not a Hallmark card, either. Love takes a concerted effort to show itself. Behind that concerted effort, is a desire to please and serve each other. Love is an encouraging word after your man has had a tough day at work. Love is a single tulip, because you know her favorite flower and you saw one on the way to pick her up. Love is the patience to allow her to study for a test, and the thoughtfulness to take her son out for ice cream so she can study uninterrupted. Love is so many beautiful, wonderful, splendid things we can share with one another. Love is not detrimental to one's character. If you are in a situation where you are being called out of your name, where you or your child is disrespected, where you are verbally, mentally or physically abused, please be aware, HE DOES NOT

LOVE YOU. In writing, if all caps is screaming, then I hope you take that as me screaming at the top of my lungs. We are all human and we will all fall short of the grace of our Creator. Regardless of that fact, that is no excuse to be abused. This book is about singles for singles, so if you are not married, you are SINGLE. There is no middle ground. I say that to emphasize, you CAN find someone better and you are not in covenant, so move toward another option. Being single and alone is better than being abused and with someone, please remember this. If you are at the point where he says he loves you, but he is abusing you or your family, he does not love you, he considers you a possession. You are not a possession. You are a person who deserves the success I am teaching in this book. Leave or get help to leave! After you are removed from the horrors of an abusive relationship, believe me you will appreciate true love in ways you cannot imagine when you are exposed to someone who will treat you as you should be treated.

To summarize, love and who you love is a choice. We (men as well), should never feel trapped to love someone. If someone feels trapped to love someone, they will wind up resenting them. Many feel the polar opposite of love is hate, but I do not completely agree. To hate someone, you have to have cared for them at some point and you are probably disgusted with something they have said or done to you. They are probably closer to you loving them again than you realize or would like to admit. I think resentment is the polar opposite of love. To resent someone is to dislike or despise who they are and how they have impacted your life. Most of the time, if someone truly harbors resentment for you, there is no turning back.

We all want to be liked, loved and sometimes we can even live with being hated so to speak, because we know at least we are on the other person's mind. No one wants to feel someone harbors resentment against them.

Now we know love is a choice. Here is my challenge to you…If you knew it, why are you still trying to love someone (or waiting for someone to love you) who has clearly shown through their actions they DO NOT love you? This is the sixty-four thousand dollar question. The answer which everyone really knows in their hearts, but often chooses to look over is: We want to feel LOVED and we want to feel like we are in LOVE. We want to experience what we believe is love and we feel as time goes on, the situation will get better. We have invested so much time and energy in this situation, at this point, we are all-in and we are "ride or die" until the end. I will talk about the "ride or die chick" later, but for now, the point is, the choice has been made, we are trying to experience love in a situation which is not conducive to what we want, what we need and what we expect it to be.

I will expound more on love being a choice as we go forward, but I want to speak for a moment about one of my experiences. I will never use real names, to protect the guilty and innocent, but if it is me which I am referring to; I will put myself on blast. I want everyone to not only learn from the knowledge I will pass along, but also from the mistakes I made.

I dated a woman for a while and after sometime and it was clear it was not going to work. I had my own issues and she did as well. I was not as financially stable as she would have liked. I did not externally show my affection for her son, as she would have liked. She could get upset about something and then stop verbally communicating with me for long stretches of time, which was extremely frustrating for me. These were some of the deal-breaking issues in that situation. Be that as it may, I loved her passionately. In my mind, she was the one and there was never any doubt. Regardless of my deep affection for her, there came a point it was clear it was over but we were kinda "hanging on" (at least I was) and she became really mean to me. This was her way of lashing out at me. She was letting me know I had really hurt her by not living up to her expectations as a significant other and no matter what I did from this point forward, my best effort to walk on egg shells around her would not be enough to avoid her wrath. For those that know me, one thing I am is persistent. Everything and everyone else be damned; I was determined to make it work. This is one of those places in life where if I could have had this insight at that time long ago, I would not have tried to continue. I could not provide what she wanted financially. I was not assuming the role of step-parent the way she would have liked it to happen. She was not helping with her attitude and the frustration in our communication. Love (especially the deep affection kind of love) has a way of making you not be able to see what is going on right before your eyes. She was beautiful, intelligent, charismatic, spiritual…everything I thought I wanted in a woman. I did want those things, but I did not know how to love *her*. Add to that the fact we had points where we could not co-exist no matter the situation. I was "hard-headed" as a child and that stubborn side can serve to be a strength and a detriment.

Here, it was definitely a detriment. Honestly, the harder I tried, the worse it got. This experience taught me I would rather swim with sharks and play with tigers and snakes rather than to truly scorn a woman. It is no joke; guys, trust me on this one. If you have not experienced it, do not go there, it is not worth it. Do not get me wrong, I take the blame for all of it. I think she is probably the sweetest woman I have ever known. She let me get to her heart, I broke it and she decided I would pay for it. I am not upset about how she treated me at this point in my life...I understand after several years, it was her way of lashing out. It was never actually personal, but it was venting...on steroids!!!

I write about this experience to bring us to the topic of our next chapter:

Chapter Two
SQUARE PEGS/ROUND HOLES

The experience I just described was literally putting a square peg into a round hole. I was so determined to make our relationship work; I could not see that I had created a situation where that relationship was beyond repair. This particular relationship would have been difficult to make work anyway. I was blinded by how I felt when everything was good with us. I could not understand that I was not working to make the relationship be what it needed to be or what it possibly could have been. By the time she had begun to lash out, we were already months past the point of no return.

No matter what we would like to believe, you cannot make a square peg fit into a round hole. If you want to get married, and one person wants to live in Sacramento, and the other wants to live in Cleveland but this issue is a deal breaker, why are you still trying to walk down the aisle? We all want to believe in the good in human nature, which is a great thing. We want to believe she will change, he will come around. NOT!!! It is not going to happen. When we are brought together, we want to believe "He loves me, we will work through this." There are places where this mindset fits. Putting the top on the toothpaste, leaving the toilet seat up, we should be able to work through those types of issues. As a matter of fact this should be a part of the things we learn to do for one another when we love each other.

What we cannot do is force someone to be someone they do not want to be and do something they do not want to do. I loved my girl…probably more than she knows to this day. What I needed to accept is that it did not matter how much I loved her, we could not work through our issues and I made it worse by staying around. Ladies, if you know you are not in a fulfilling relationship and you are working to make it fulfilling, and either (a) he is not working to make it fulfilling or (b) he has/is working to make it fulfilling but you have exhausted every option; you have come to a point where it is time to let go. Sometimes it is ok, to say "I love you, but I cannot be with you." I think our Creator made us incompatible with some people for several reasons. One very important reason is we have to learn from life experiences how to treat someone properly. If I did not learn anything from the relationship I talked about in chapter one, it was pointless. I know there is not one second in my life which was meant to be pointless. I learned how to listen, how to find the cues when my woman is speaking to me in the language she wants me to hear in. Many times, guys, a woman can be reaching out to us, but we really do not hear it. There is a book called "The Five Love Languages," by Dr. Gary Chapman. I suggest, recommend and beg of you, whatever I need to do to get you to read this book. Dr. Chapman has pinpointed how we communicate, in the ways we want to give and receive love from one another. If you do not know how your significant other is trying to talk to you (ladies, this is for you as well), you will never be able to communicate clearly with them. I will explore that as we get into the concept of the nine tenets. I say that to touch on the fact I had to learn how to communicate with my woman on every level. Knowing what she expects makes the battle no longer a battle; it makes it working on a life together.

I would like to expound a bit more on the square peg/round hole phenomena. We can be extremely determined to make a relationship work, therefore sometimes we can actually see it will not work, but we envision what it *could* be. Many times we do not see the relationship for what it is and we try to force it. Here is an example of trying to force something to work which is clearly not going to work. On another occasion, I dated a woman who again, I was very attached to. I had love for her and I believe she did for me as well. I will speak to what we can and cannot deal with later in the book, but she had a trait I simply could not deal with. Her personality made it very difficult for her to let go of her past. I believe in many ways, she was scarred, which is not fair to her and unfortunate to say the least. Regardless of that characteristic in her, to have a life with me, that was something that was non-negotiable. I tried to give her time to work through it but it was not happening quickly enough. She had to let the past go, or we could not move forward. The fact of the matter is, maybe one day she will (or has at this point) let the past go. At that time she could not let it go, and was not willing to make a concerted effort to try to move on. That is not necessarily right or wrong, it is what it is. The problem is, that does not work for me, so ultimately, we could not be together. No matter what I felt for her, or she felt for me, I could not get past how I felt about that trait. I knew I could not deal with it. I tried to make it work anyway. I tried to go back and make it work, even after we had split. I think I tried again and we split again. I knew I was diggin' her, but when this one thing popped up, I could not deal. It was a deal-breaker for me. Why keep putting this beautiful, intelligent, caring, considerate woman through this, for the selfish reason of "I believe I can make it work?" Most of my mistakes in relationships, I can charge to youth or ignorance. I wish I could say that here, but in this case, it was plain stupidity and selfishness on my part. It would not work, it was never going to work and I knew it but my determination, perseverance and persistence which normally serve me well, worked against me this time. No matter what I did, I was never going to be able to put that square peg of my conscience into the round hole of our relationship.

There is a moral here beyond simple application of this philosophy: Ladies and Gentlemen, please do not try to fight through a deal-breaker. We will have inconveniences in life which are not necessarily deal-breakers. Again, leaving the top off of the toothpaste, deciding who will wash dishes, who will pick up the mail, or drop off the dry cleaning, these situations to most people would simply be inconveniences. It takes patience and understanding to realize we have all been raised differently, which evolved into we all live differently as adults. It will take time to work through the nuances of each other. When a couple is dating, this is a great time to work through the nuances you can learn about each other, within the context of dating. If you take the time to learn what you really like and really do not care for in each other, you can begin to work through them together before you say "I do." A couple does not have to live together to learn what each other's likes and dislikes are. You will not learn everything, but you will learn enough to know what you can and cannot live with. Learning inconveniences or differences early and being able to see them for what they are and that they are not going to change (or working them out together) is the way to alleviate blow ups over "little things" once you get married. It is ok to see your significant other through rose colored glasses, but be wise enough to take them off long enough to learn their quirks or nuances are, so you will not make them into deal-breakers. Once you know what their nuances are, you will not see that nuance as "the straw that broke the camel's back" during an argument. You already knew it was a part of who they were when you declared your love for each other on your wedding day. Deal-breakers are different things for different people. Sometimes a deal-breaker may be that one party or the other does not want kids and is not willing to budge. It could be that someone cannot leave a city for a certain reason, or they cannot go to another level with you because of a family tradition or heritage. There are times when the deal-breaker is more subtle: They may be someone you love, but they are indifferent to everything. They can go to any movie, any restaurant, they just cannot make a decision on which one, and they always leave that up to you. That can be a legitimate deal-breaker! Everyone will have different characteristics they can and cannot live with, and it is up to each of us to look for that when we are dating and assess if it is an inconvenience or a deal-breaker. If it is a deal breaker, understand that sometimes it is ok to say, "I love you, but you have to be you and this does not work for me right now." Please hear me on this point. If it is meant to be, it will be. If someone does something they feel pressured to do, it will not be out of love but out of being compelled or pushed to feel a certain way. A relationship based on a person being pressured to do something is destined to fail. A relationship that is supposed to happen will happen. The fact you did what you should have done at this crucial point will make it even more beautiful if you are destined to get back together. You cannot stop destiny…you cannot even contain it! Do what you know is right for you, your significant other and the situation; and the rest will work out the way it is supposed to.

Chapter Three
KNOWING YOURSELF

This may be the most challenging chapter in this book for some. The reality is many of us do not know ourselves. We do not know ourselves, so we cannot love ourselves. Since we do not love ourselves, how can we love anyone else, or let anyone else love us? Have you experienced life on your own? Have you experienced the things which truly make you happy? I have a friend who I asked if it would it make her happy if I took to her shopping on Rodeo Drive in Beverly Hills. She told me, no, if we visit California she would rather visit the Redwood Forest. Wow! That is a revelation to me about her. The real point here is it is not a revelation to her, because she knows herself. Do not be mistaken here, she dresses well and likes to be "cute," but she is more interested in nature than shopping. Now I know there are some guys out there who are tired of shopping and are looking for my email address at this very moment to inquire about my friend. Unfortunately as of the writing of this book, she is taken.

It is important to understand the depth of my friend. She is a considerate, giving person. She is also uncompromising on her ethical standards. She has a sense of her self-worth, and she realizes her value to those in her life. Many ladies I know do not realize how important they are. I can say this woman realizes that importance, which gives her a sense of confidence that is important in every facet of life. You can see it the way she carries herself and in the way she speaks. She has been blessed to have a high-earning career through hard work and making good life choices. She is humbled by her blessing, but by her knowing intimately who she is, and who she looks to for everything (her Creator), she is unapologetic for the life she lives. Although I doubt any of us have moments where we have not wavered on faith, her foundation in her life is her faith in Christ. The fact my friend knows who she is allows her to know what she wants, and what she is capable of dealing with. Most importantly, knowing herself allows her to be compromising only when it makes sense to her, as opposed to those who compromise who they are for the sake of others because of their lack of self-worth.

We have to learn to understand ourselves and take the time to know what we like and what we do not like. As individuals, we have to deal with stereotypes associated with culture, religion, gender, ethnicity and even region of the country one lives in. Although some of those things can be found to be true, we are individuals with our own hearts, minds, thoughts, feelings and desires. I want to show each of you how to translate the right information to those who we are in relationships with or to those we want to have relationships with. To translate those factors, we need to learn them ourselves. Let me frame some examples.

First of all, I do not know anyone who does not like to travel. I am certain some people do not, but my inner circle of friends and family love to travel. Although that is the case, I have one friend who hates to fly. For him to travel on a plane, it is a different situation, different mindset than for most of us. He has to be extra-committed to what he is doing and where he is going. Undoubtedly, he understands this about himself and those around him understand it. To get him to get on an airplane may be more difficult than getting Mr. T on the A-team to fly. It is close to a deal-breaker for him, so someone in a relationship with him needs to understand this about him. The bigger picture is, he knows his limitations and he works within those parameters, so those around him have to respect his limitations as well.

Secondly, I have another friend in a relevant situation…we will call her Janet. Janet is in love with being in love. She wants someone to love her more than even I can understand. She is a caring mom, a divorcee and even beyond this, she has a heart of gold to everyone who comes in contact with her. Janet is affectionate. Adding to that affection, she is one who gets "sprung" fairly quickly. Of course, this is because she loves being in love. When I talk to her about her situations, I always try to make her understand the element of what the person she is trying to date is trying to accomplish. Sometimes this is challenging for her, because she so desperately wants to find true happiness and experience what love is supposed to feel like…what she envisions love to feel like. What I try to communicate to Janet is to learn what she likes and what she does not like. I asked her what she wants out of a relationship. Janet replied, "For someone to be romantic, as I am a romantic person and for me to experience what that would be like. I want someone to be there for me, like I have been there for them. I have never had someone be romantic to me and I would like to experience that." I am a sucker for romance, so I admire this way of thinking. The challenge I have with Janet wanting to experience romance is she is using the thought of romance as a substitute for love. She definitely wants romance, no question, but the love she wants is the basis for the romance. I would like to see her prepare for the love and romance by developing herself. There is an old adage and I will paraphrase, "Somewhere, God is preparing your man/woman for you right now." I believe this is absolutely true. I also feel God is working in us to prepare for the mate to come. I want to see Janet work to prepare for the inevitability of having a beautiful relationship. She will bring a well-rounded woman to the table in the future and she will get better results. I want her to go out and do some things on her own. She likes to travel, but does not get to travel very often...so she should find a spot and take a trip. She likes to write, so maybe she should find a writers group to join, or something of that nature. Janet is such a giving person, often she gives all of herself and there is nothing left for her. She has to learn about herself, what she has to offer, what she wants out of life and that it is ok to do things for yourself. As she grows and develops into a well-rounded person and knows herself better, she will bring more substance to that beautiful "match made in Heaven" when it begins to develop. With this growth she will learn to be clear in her communication with her man and it will be clear to her partner what she wants and needs. Janet will probably have to get him to slow down on the romance once she knows how to give the right signals to get what she wants. Right now, she cannot see what she does not want in a man, until she is so caught up emotionally, it is tough to let go. I must give her kudos, she does have the capability to cut someone off when necessary, but that is only after she has almost made it to the point of resentment. It is not healthy for us to have to wait until someone has disappointed us so much to the point we have to cut them off. If he is not romantic and affectionate and it is still in the first month, Babi girl…he will never be! Do not settle with that person, if romance is something your heart desires. Send him on his way to his blessing and continue working on yourself until you find yours. There is definitely a light at the end of the tunnel—it's a train! There is no sense in waiting to get knocked off of the tracks to be pissed off—get out of the way! Knowing herself better will allow her to find someone to love her for whom she truly is and she can stop accepting applications from those who are clearly unqualified from the beginning.

From what we have learned in this chapter, let's assume that we know ourselves. To recap a bit, knowing yourself would include knowing what makes you happy, what things in life you want to accomplish, what your desires are, and a general, overall sense of self. Also, for the purpose of this book, knowing yourself would entail knowing what you want out of a relationship at this moment in time and what your expectations are for the future in the relationship. This is a great start. Now that we know ourselves, we accept who we are, we are comfortable with our character, we work to continue to strive to be the best individual we can be and we are happy with who we are. So loving this person should be a breeze, right? I have to say most of the people I know would say they love themselves, but I would say approximately less than half show it. If you love yourself, treat yourself as such. Make it a point to make time for yourself. If you have children, taking a moment out for yourself is not as though you stopped taking care of them. Keep in mind, you need "me time" so you can stay refreshed as a parent. Ladies, do not wait for a man to pamper you, be willing to pamper yourself. If it is a spa day, a yoga class, or just taking some time to go to the park and read a good book, you have to be willing to treat yourself as though you love yourself. Physically, spiritually, emotionally and mentally. Love yourself enough to be happy with you are and then you will be enlightened to see how easy it is for someone else to love you and treat you the way you should be treated. Guys, you have to be willing to find things that are fulfilling to you as well. For us, showing ourselves some love may just be allowing ourselves to let go of work for a while, when we get home. It could be something as drastic as fulfilling an adventurous dream you have always wanted to do (skydiving, parasailing, or driving a race car), or as subtle as taking a mission trip or helping someone build a home. As a bit of a sidenote, we should all take note it is amazing how much we feel love when we have an opportunity to help others…even those we do not know.

The image we present to others plays into how we feel about ourselves as well. If you need some clothes, but you want to keep the children looking good, that is great and it can be done without breaking the bank. Save some money specifically for you, shop smart, and make sure you are dressing well also. I notice in both men and women, when we are looking on point, we carry ourselves differently. I have seen it in my co-workers, friends, family, etc. The better you feel about the way you are dressed, the better you feel about yourself. You exude more confidence. You tend to stand up straighter, you tend to look people in the eye and smile more; even if you do not normally carry yourself this way. Again, love is a verb disguised as a noun. You have to show love for yourself as well as others. When you make an effort to do and achieve the things that make you feel good about yourself, you will work to show you feel good about yourself as well. Do not get me wrong, this is not about things, this is about an individual showing they care enough about their own well being to treat themselves to the things they desire in life. That leads me to share this next experience.

I have a friend, we will call her Persia. Persia is attractive. Long legs, pretty smile…very attractive, professional woman. Persia and I would hang out and do things together. She has always had a perception of herself that she was ok, but not a knockout, so she would be happy where she was with what she had. Babi girl (this phrase is my term of endearment, if you have not figured it out by now) had a cool little ride, paid for, four door. It was not anything too over the top, nothing too fancy but economical on gas and reliable. It was a little older and maybe she was thinking it was time to step it up. She decided she wanted to do it kinda big for her standards and drive a car which some people would think of as a status symbol. She buys the car, gets lots of compliments and people are showing her love about it. I notice a change in her demeanor but not in a bad way. She simply became even more personable than before. Persia decided to change her style a bit. She changed her hairstyle and then she went shopping. Bam! Where did this girl come from? Did I know her? Now she has guys hitting on her left and right and they have not seen her new car or know anything about it. It started with her loving herself enough to make herself happy. It is not about going in a mountain of debt to be ballin' so to speak…that is not what I'm talking about. It is about loving yourself enough to do what it takes to make yourself happy. In this case, it was a physical change. We are not here to live for the stuff we can get, but there is a place for the desires of your heart. A relationship with the Creator should be the first desire. It is still ok to change things around you (within reason) to make it a point to love one's self. Not because of the car, but because of the change in attitude, Persia still carries this confidence around like she had it from day one. Her perception of herself has changed and now it is clear the perception of those around her has changed as well…in a good way. I am a Lamborghini fan. I do not have Gallardo money. Am I mistreating myself because I do not own an Italian sports car? No. I make that statement to reiterate, this is not about money or stuff. The idea is to find what really makes you happy inside and work to fulfill that happiness, that true desire. The point is find the things in life that make you happy, whatever they are; travel, helping others, sports cars, clothing, day spas, hiking, bird-watching, ice-skating, writing, singing, nature walks…whatever it may be which truly makes you happy; go for it! Life is definitely about the journey. I will touch on that more later, but directing the journey to the next plateau in life around what you want to reach or achieve is actually a way of loving yourself daily.

Now, let us get into the heart of the matter. You have the foundation. It is time to build the character of a successful relationship.

Chapter Four

NOTHING WORTH HAVING IS EASY

We have built the foundation for successful relationships. You should always remember to make good choices, do not try to force something which is not there and finally, know and love yourself. These are the basics. This is the groundwork. Keep in mind, once the groundwork is laid, it must be maintained. Analyze your choices from a common sense perspective. If something is working, build on it, if not, move on and build a new foundation elsewhere. Maintain your mental, spiritual, physical and emotional health. Energize and motivate yourself by doing the things for you which make your spirit flourish and make you feel everyday is a day the Creator has made especially for you.

When I was a very young child, my grandfather had a garden. It was very large, probably two or three acres. He would grow corn, tomatoes, squash, green beans, turnips and many other vegetables. He would work very hard to make sure the garden was well cultivated. He would have me, as a three-year-old, riding a tractor with him while he was plowing the garden. I remember having the time of my life, enjoying being with Granddaddy, "driving" the tractor. I had no idea what we were doing was so vital to how the crop would eventually turn out. In comparison, plowing the field was easier as opposed to him teaching me to sow seeds, or tie tomato plants, or other things necessary to make a garden grow properly. Although mundane, plowing the field was necessary. None of the other things we did later would have mattered if we had not worked very hard to make sure the land was properly cultivated. This applies to most facets of life and it especially applies to relationships. If a relationship is not properly cultivated, it will not thrive, just like a garden not properly cultivated will not produce a good harvest. This brings us to the first tenet of a successful relationship:

Tenet #1: Work on Your Relationship Constantly for it to Thrive

If I were writing these tenets as components of a *Billboard* Music Chart, this tenet would be number one, with a bullet (which means, it is number one and STILL climbing). I am guilty of not working on a relationship. I do not know one person who at some point has not been guilty of letting their relationship ride on cruise control, at least for some amount of time. Do not feel like you are in a minority if you currently fit in this category, or have fit in this category. Many people believe relationships just happen, that they simply "evolve." Relationships do not evolve; they grow from the seeds planted by the people in the relationship. If you do not make significant contributions to the relationship, you will not see significant rewards. Think of a relationship as an investment in you and your significant other. Your return on investment will look like the stock market in 2008 (horrific) if you do not evaluate your relationship, be prepared to plant the necessary seeds and put in the time and effort to cultivate growth.

The opportunity to work on your relationship is a blessing, not a curse. I often hear people complaining about what their mate is asking of them, or they are complaining about what their expectation of their mate is. Let me paint a picture for you: If you date your spouse before you get married, at some point, the true person starts to come out. Most relationships begin with the person's "representative" being introduced to one another. Here are examples of the common male and female "representative." The male representative would be the cool dude you met in the beginning. He bought you a drink or danced with you, spit a little game to you and next thing you know, you have given him your email address, shoe size, social and of course-your phone number. So ladies, now you think you have the best guy since sliced bread. He knows how to talk to you, he knows how to say just the right thing at the right time and he makes your heart skip a beat every time you see him or talk to him. It is great that you like him, but enjoy this part of him while it lasts, because most of the time, the representative will stay around until they find out if you are truly mate material. If they simply want a physical relationship, they may stay around long enough to try to see if they can get what they want and then "all of a sudden" he becomes a different person. One common version of the person who only wants a physical relationship will only call when he wants you physically. Then and only then will he call. I want you to be aware of what you are seeing when you are blinded by love, lust and some variation of hormones interfering with the way you would normally think. The ladies have a representative, too. Quite often, when you see a lady in a setting of her choice, she is dressed well, sophisticated, Miss Independent. One could easily get the sense that she does not need a man. She is a lady who can take care of herself. Most men (myself included) like the challenge of the woman who has every-thing, but does not need me. What guy would not want this woman to want him? Her representative is a challenge to a guy and not to mention a very enticing characteristic. I speak of the representatives so we understand what we are really experiencing in the early stages of the relationship. The representative may stay around for three months, maybe as much as six months. However long it takes to begin to feel comfortable with one another. Eventually, after the first disagreement or the first truly tough moment they experience together, they are now comfortable enough with one another for the representative to leave. The real person has entered the relationship. You will get to know them quicker than you expect. Once she is comfortable, she wants you to go grocery shopping with her, cut her lawn, or wash her car. Once he is comfortable, he will want you cook for him, clean his house or simply let him watch the game uninterrupted.

As you get deeper into the relationship, you learn what your expectations are of each other. Some things you are kinda cool with, other things you do not like and there are some things you despise. By now, you have both said you love one another more than once. I will reiterate the following thought throughout the book. Love is a verb disguised as a noun. You love her/him, so the things you agree to do for one another; you do them out of love. Do not do them with a spiteful heart. The opportunity to work for your mate is a blessing. This is the person you want to be with, the one God divinely put in place for you. This does not mean to be foolish or be a doormat and let the other person walk over you. Know how to set reasonable boundaries and expectations you can follow. We each know what we can and cannot accept doing for each other. That being said, the things you agree to do for your mate, they are a blessing; for those things are the way you show your love to the one you care for more than anyone else on this Earth. In those fleeting moments when you hate washing her car, remember the look on her face and how happy she will be when you bring it home to her. When you are cleaning his house, remember how happy he will be when he sees what you did for him, because you love him.

When you have a relationship, or when you are married, you are working to make each other happy and content. It should be a joy to make your spouse/boo happy, literally. It should not be a deplorable task each and every day. In the relationship I spoke about in chapter one, we had a two-part relationship. Part one was before the breakup; part two was the reconciliation. A great example of working through challenges was dealing with the trash. I loathed taking out the trash. I cannot remember perfectly, but I am pretty sure, when I was growing up I never had to do it. I was expected to take out the trash in part one. I am not sure why, but I hated taking out the trash. I really would not let it get out of hand by having many, many bags to dump at once, but I never liked it. Although I did not mind alternating who would take out the garbage in part one, I was reluctant-scratch that…*I was not having it* as far as me taking out the trash every time. She grew up where men took out the trash. "Great," I would think to myself, "she should call one of them over when it is her turn, and they can get it for her," I would think to myself *aloud*. I learned by the time we got to part two, this was close to a deal-breaker for her. If I was going to show my love *as a verb*, I needed to get with this garbage thing. I still did not like doing it, but if it made my boo happy, her happiness made me happy. I did not do it with a spiteful heart (as may have possibly happened before). I did it out of love and I would do it again. That is the kind of uncon-ditional love you must have for your spouse. You want to love them to a point where you will do things you would not normally choose to do to make them happy and more importantly, you do those things from a place of love. For example, if you know your man hates balancing the checkbook, but you are good at it and you can do it effectively, take it off of his plate every now and then. He will appreciate you for it and he will remember he is with you because you love him. You will want to do things to show him you love him, long after your "representative" has left the relationship.

I want to put a footnote of sorts to this chapter. This is about where I introduce, "The Sucka Move." Guys, we catch it from our friends sometimes for doing what our ladies ask us to do (some ladies do as well from their friends). Do not fall victim to this. This is a "Sucka Move." Misery loves company. There are guys out there who would enjoy entertaining themselves with your story of how you had to sleep on the couch, or some other foolishness, after they told you to "man up" and "wear the pants." This will be the same person that has no woman, or has a terrible relationship, so you may as well "hate on women" together as far as he is concerned. The intelligent man who wears the pants in the family does what his spouse needs him to do. If you need to do something for your lady and it is understood you will take care of it then it needs to be a priority. Why go home to an unhappy house, because you wanted to stay another hour with your boys, but you missed picking up her dry cleaning? Was that move really worth the three days of berating comments, evil looks, and lack of intimacy you will undoubtedly experience? More importantly, you want to make her happy, right? Do what you gotta do to make her happy, she will go the extra mile to make you happy. It may not seem fair that you have to go above and beyond initially, but life is not fair, so hear me when I say this—work constantly to make your woman happy and you will have a great life together. Keep your lady happy and she will make you feel like the center of her universe.

Chapter Five

THAT IS NOT WHAT I THOUGHT
YOU SAID

You talk about a great many things over the course of a day, to a great many people. You talk to your mate in the morning about getting ready for work, what the plan is for the day and hopefully you tell them you love them in some way as you separate and leave each other's presence for the day. Then, you have to talk to co-workers about work, speak to the boss about what is on your agenda for the day or week and maybe talk to customers, vendors, merchants, peers, management and associates throughout the day. There is a good chance you will talk to a friend, maybe during lunch, on a break or some other point during the course of the day. When you return home, you will speak with family and possibly friends and acquaintances, before you start a new day. This is an over-simplified way of magnifying how much you communicate and how important it is to communicate through-out any given day. Communication is the single most highly-used, under-valued component in any relationship. Tenet number two is a very important tenet:

Tenet #2: Communicate Clearly and Effectively
with Your Mate

This tenet should have a subtitle. The subtitle would read: "Do Not Leave Room for Misinterpretation." Let us talk about exactly this point-misinterpretation. Here is a quick example of how this is detrimental to a relationship. I was dating a young lady several years ago. I will refer to her as "Tonya." Tonya was a very nice woman, but we never communicated on the same level from the beginning. Our needs, expectations and desires out of life and each other never seemed to be communicated properly, from either of us. She seemed to want a relationship with me; as a matter of fact, she pursued me. The problem was, when we started dating, we never were on the same path. If I expected to go out on a certain day, inevitably Tonya had other plans. If Tonya wanted to spend time with me, I was tired from work or something else was going on. We could never make the other person understand our intentions. We dated for about three months, and it easily could have ended much earlier. We were both good people, with good hearts and good intentions…they just never properly intertwined for our relationship to work.

I learned an important lesson from that situation. Make sure your mate understands what you want and need from the relationship. Everyone has strengths and weaknesses. Some will be great communicators and some will not. If you are good at communicating, that will help you as you go along. If your partner does not communicate well, you can teach them some ways to communicate to help you understand each other better. If you are not a good communicator…well, let me see what I can do to keep you from wasting three months (or more) like I did.

Communication comes in many forms. Verbal communication is important and in my experience, it is the way men communicate the most. We also communicate in the actions we perform for and with one another. The things we do for and with one another within the context of a relationship speak volumes. Often, actions speak much more than words ever could say. When your mate needs something they cannot get on their own, if you can get it, or you can be a resource to find a way to get it; take the initiative and make it happen. Doing for your mate when they cannot do for themselves shows your love and the quality of your thoughtfulness when it comes to your mate. Doing for your mate is what a relationship is really about.

In the following paragraphs, there is an example of where there is something "lost in translation" and here is an example of learning to communicate effectively.

I will refer to the relationship where I describe there is a part 1 and part 2 several times, because I learned a lot of lessons I want to pass along from that experience. During part 2 of that experience, I can remember mowing the lawn a few times. When I was a child, I mowed our lawn a lot. As soon as I was old enough (twelve), I would go around to neighbors, and try to find out who would like for me to mow their lawn for a small fee. I had my first job and I was very happy about it. I used the money to buy baseball cards and other things a twelve-year-old baseball and football fan would buy. What I did not realize at the time was that I had seasonal allergies which always appear in Spring. Looking back, I can remember a little coughing, clearing the throat and sneezing when I was cutting grass, but I did not let it stop me. After playing football and basketball outdoors for several years, I realized my allergies were more of a problem than I thought. Freshly mowed grass never helped my allergies. Basically, between the allergies and my father deciding he was not trying to share the responsibility of mowing our lawn from time to time, I decided once I was old enough, I would not be mowing anymore. Fast forward to part two of my relationship. I wanted to pay to have the lawn cut, but money was tight sometimes, so I bought a lawn mower. I can remember my boo telling me about how meticulous her Dad cut their grass when she was growing up. He did it so perfectly; it was almost funny to her. Only after we were long since broken up, did I figure out she was trying to communicate on another level. There was a day I remember quite well. She was normally gone on Saturday mornings to get her hair done and I mowed the lawn on a few of those mornings. This particular Saturday morning, she did not go to the salon and I got up and cut the grass. I remember seeing her, as she watched me cut it almost the entire time from the living room window and kitchen window. I remember wondering, "Why is she watching me? Is she enjoying seeing me do some manual labor for a change?" I was pouring with sweat, eyes watering from my allergies, on alert for hidden rocks in the ground trying to destroy my mower and I was clearly not happy. Only years later, did the vision of her watching what was going on come back to me. She was seeing me work with a smile on her face. I remember she offered me water two or three times and happily continued to enjoy my work as she watched me work. It made her happy for me to do something she wanted to have done. She told me she wanted to feel secure. For me to do things she was used to a man doing made her feel secure. It took me a long time to understand how these things made her feel. Although, I did not know it at the time, the way I was communicating was effective. The things I spoke of (dumping trash, mowing lawn) were ways of communicating my love to her.

Find ways to serve and assist in your relationship as a component of communicating your love. Women want to feel secure and provided for. I can attest to the fact I did not do that in the examples of taking out the trash and mowing the lawn (during the times where I did not want to do it). Society has set an expectation that women are equal to men in every way. I am not the right person to comment on that but women are definitely different than men, this much I can comment on. Different especially in the ways in which they communicate. Women communicate they want security in subtle ways, quite often. They may show they want show they want security in the area they want to live, the type of car they want to drive or in how much/what types of ways they want to save money. Guys, we have to look at context clues in her words and actions to hear what she is saying. If you hear your woman say, "I have read reviews on this SUV, and it seems to be very safe," that means she is interested in having a safe vehicle to drive. This sounds like overstating the obvious, but when you compare it to a man's similar commentary on vehicles "I hear the new Porsche truck does 0-60 in 4.9 seconds and is the fastest truck ever tested on the skid pad," it's fairly obvious men do not often talk about cars in the context of security. Guys tend to talk about cars with more of a "fantasy of being a race car driver/death wish" in mind. This is an example of being able to recognize someone is communicating about security, but we need to be aware of whatever she is communicating about through the content and context of her conversation. Ladies, guys are a bit more upfront about what they want and desire. Ladies have to understand for the most part guys will tell you what they want through verbal communication. If you listen to what he says and take it for what it is worth, you will usually know how to serve and assist him as a way of communicating your love to him.

The example I gave with "Tonya" is an example of literally two people communicating often, but no matter the style or format of the communication, everything we said or did was lost in translation. Here is a similar situation. I know someone from what seems like "a past life." We have so many things in common. We love to debate all sorts of topics, we dig world issues, we can talk sports and we have a shared spirituality. All those things being what they are, when we tried to communicate on an intimate level, it is as if we were from different islands on different sides of the world. We share a love for our spiritual beliefs, but they could not be more far apart. I talked about maybe one day having a family; she talked about not wanting so much as a goldfish. I am a romantic, she is anti-pda (personal displays of affection), anti-flowers of any kind and basically anti-affectionate in many ways. The kicker is she will "go hard" on me and call me a punk—because of my affectionate personality. We have all the characteristics of a match made in Heaven, but there is a lot which is lost in translation between us. The good thing is we both recognized it, and it never went far enough for either of us to get hurt or disappointed. We simply remained friends.

If you are in a relationship and you can see there are places where you are losing one another in translation, do not give up. In my previous case, we realized there was just too much that did not translate to a romantic relationship, but that is not always the case. The first thing to do is recognize you are not seeing eye to eye and look for where the disconnect is. Once you pinpoint the disconnect, talk it through. After you discuss it and have found a common ground, the key is to make the expectations clear to one another. For example: "If you do X, and I do Y, we can meet at Z." When you have this understanding, have your mate communicate it back to you. Now you have found the disconnect, closed the gap, set an expectation for one another and finally repeated it to one another so you each know there is nothing lost in translation. This refers back to "Do Not Leave Room for Misinterpretation." Make your intentions as clear as a traffic signal. My eight-year-old will say, "Daddy, the light is green," if I sit at a light too long and it has changed from red to green. Even she knows a green light means go. When communicating to your mate, be like the traffic light—be clear. Make your intentions overtly clear but do this with sincerity and from a place of love. Do not allow yourself to come off condescending to prove a point. Just as it is a blessing to do things for your mate, it is also a blessing to know you understand each other. Do not take communication with your mate for granted, take it as another step in your successful walk with your boo.

Some of my examples have been challenging to say the least. This one speaks to how communicating the right way from the beginning makes things so much smoother. One of my friends has been married for a few years. He goes out with me and the rest of our crew from time to time. I must preface a little about him. Growing up, he had two great women in his life, his mom and grandmother. I had an awesome grandmother in my life as well. I was simply stubborn and hard-headed; therefore I had to learn through experience, so the result is this book for you. On the other hand, he was obviously paying closer attention when growing up. He saw what they liked, appreciated, wanted, needed and deserved. He took these cues into his relationship. Interestingly enough, he dated his lady for a while before they were married and even when they were well past the "representative" stage; he would do things I rarely did. I never saw my other friends do any of those things at all. If we were at a restaurant, he would call and ask his lady if she wanted something to eat. I would say 90% of the time, she would say no, but he called and asked all the time. If she wanted something and he could get it, or find a resource to get it, he would make it happen. The key here is not what he did; it is when and where he did it. She was always a top priority to him, regardless of what he was doing, where he was, or who he was with. If she wanted some-thing, he was going to make it happen. Most importantly, even when he could not make it happen at the moment, he would make mental notes and make it happen at some point. There was verbal communication in asking what she wanted. The bigger picture is the non-verbal communication of satisfying a want or need. Even when it was not at the top of her mind at the moment, her wants and needs were still at the top of his mind. We can all learn to make communicating with our mate a top priority at *all* times and making it happen by serving and assisting becomes much easier for all of us to do.

Communicate clearly and effectively and avoid the drama which will most certainly follow the comment, "that is not what I thought you said."

Chapter Six

LOVE IS A STUPID DRUG

This is definitely the topic in my book which gives me the most disappointment in other people's relationships. This is probably the topic which a lot of men will immediately understand and appreciate but not so much with women. My goal is for everyone to leave this chapter appreciating their opinions and beliefs even more than they already do.

I write this with the belief that we value ourselves highly. I am speaking for myself when I say I value my opinion but I believe we all value our opinions. I have learned over the years, it is not enough to make judgments and decisions based on what I see on the surface, about anything. I always want to make an informed opinion. Some things will require more research than others, but the bottom line is: I need to take the time to know what I am talking about when I want to share an opinion on something. This opinion may or may not be worth anything to anyone but me, but I have the facts and information to back up what I say. I used to not always take the time to do this. I would use half the facts, but would want to form an entire opinion. Well, that is fine when you are talking to someone who does not understand something as well as you do. When you do share an opinion with someone who is well-informed and you are either half informed, or misinformed; your opinion becomes less valid, in the eyes of others.

This being what it is, we all have opinions on relationships. We all have friends who come to us for help. We have family who comes to us for help. Whether we are relationship experts or not, it is often easier for someone on the outside to have more clarity in someone else's relationship, than it is for the person in the relationship. Their judgment can be clouded by love, closeness to the situation, family pressure, family traditions and a host of other things which can make their decision making seem poor. This is why we often look to someone outside of the relationship for clarity. This brings us to tenet number three:

Tenet #3: Do Not Do Anything You Would Not Advise a Friend to Do

This is not the first tenet, but it is definitely Relationship 101 material. The genders tend to have different strengths and weaknesses. I have found with my friends, the guys tend not to have as much of a problem with this tenet. They are not perfect with it, but they are more in line with this way of thinking than ladies are. The ladies tend to have a different rationale here and I want to touch on that method of thinking.

First of all, very simply stated, if you would advise someone else against doing something you are currently doing; that should sound an alarm in your mind. It should, at the very least, make you re-evaluate your situation.

I want to start with a high-profile situation. I should preface, if you haven't figured it out, I like sports cars. Very superficial or whatever one would like to call it, but I drive a sports car, and I am a passionate sports car buff, so a sports car or several might be referred to in my analogies. I make no bones about it…Lord-willing, there is a blue Gallardo in my future with a Crème-colored interior. In 2009, the Lamborghini logo was totally disrespected by two high profile celebrities who decided to fight in a Lambo (a Gallardo on top of that!). It was a young man and a young lady, and although at the time of this writing, there has been no final assessment, something happened in the car where the young lady was clearly beaten pro-fusely. I cannot tell you what specifically happened, I was not there but I know this girl was clearly battered and from looking at one photo, beyond recognition. Not too long after the incident, the couple got back together. They have since been pushed apart, most likely due to public pressure, internal team pressure and also a court order. I have been talking to a friend about this situation and we shared how we thought it would go. She said she thought they were done, there was no way they would reconcile, as it would probably simply be more of a public relations nightmare and cause further damage to both of their careers than reconciliation would be worth. I said, I felt if she loved him (which I don't know her personally, just an observation from a distance), she would not let him go that easily and they would reconcile, at least for a while. I felt she would give him the benefit of the doubt. I am sure I am wrong quite often, but this time I was right, at least initially as they did get back together for a bit. My friend sent me a text saying they were back together. I responded, saying I was not surprised. I told my friend, "Love is a drug." She texted me back, "Love is a stupid drug." I remember thinking about that phrase that day. My friend was spot on in her text. Love is more powerful than any narcotic; it will make you do things you never believed you would do. I can attest to this. I have had a dose or two of "stupid." I can remember crying for hours at a time, because I loved someone, but I was not sure if they loved me or if they even cared about me. The crying was a release I suppose but in hindsight, was it really necessary to get caught up for hours, which turned into days, which turned into months? I was never depressed. I just was distraught on whether or not I would experience the love I had before and wanted so much to have again. There is a time to grieve…even a relationship. There is also a time to move on. It is difficult to set that timetable for ourselves, but we have to know when enough is enough. At some point, one must let go and move on.

I have a sensitive, emotional side but you would never catch me showing signs of my pain in public. While I was dealing with the situation I just spoke of, you would have never known I was going through it if I did not want you to know. It is like, I was a function-ing junkie. Love will do this to you, if you do not take a minute to control it, as opposed to it controlling you.

My grandmother was a very plain-spoken woman. When giving me advice, she was a woman of very few words. If my grandmother would have been able to, as she was in her last year with us while I was going through this, I am sure she would have said, "Boy, get over it…you will find another girl." She never had the chance to tell me that. It probably would have been the detox I needed.

I talk about that example to say, I had friends who talked to me during this time. They knew what I was going through. One of my partners did as I would have done for him; he kept it real with me. He said, "You messed it up, you cannot fix it, it is too late. Let it go and find someone else." I did not single-handedly mess things up but the honesty of a relationship is you learn to take responsibility for your own actions. If I had not done my part in damaging the relationship, we probably could have worked through the rest. Therefore, it is my fault, I take the blame and he is correct. Now, here is where I did not understand this tenet at the time. Do not do something you would not advise a friend to do. I wanted to make it work. I wanted to keep the idea in my mind this was going to work out. I prayed over the course of the year following the break-up probably more than I had prayed in my thirty-something years before the break-up combined. The Lord is probably tired of hearing my voice, I prayed so much. I heard someone say that sometimes rejection is God's protection. I know that applied in this situation now. I simply chose to live in the grieving phase much longer than I should have. If I would have taken a moment and stepped away from the closeness I had to the situation, I could have saved myself recurring heartbreak for about a year. I would have never advised one of my daughters to allow themselves to marinate in this pain for a week, never mind a year. I would have never advised a friend to go through what I was going through; especially while having the control to change their perspective (as I did). I do not think we ever stop loving someone we truly love. We can, however, love them from a distance and let go of torturing ourselves about something which is no longer a part of our life. If I could not advise a friend to go through this…why in the world would I allow myself to go through this? Lesson learned…never again! My opinion of other relationships is valid; why would I not allow my opinion to be unbiased for a moment and validate itself? Because I was so close to the situation and I did not want to take anything else for an answer other than what I wanted. What you want may not be what you need. Step away from situations and advise yourself accordingly. Think about the situation and ask yourself what you would tell your friend to do, if this were a friend's situation. There is your answer you have been so desperately searching for. Also, let me reiterate, His protection may be a rejection you do not want to accept, but may be best for you so be open to it. You are the best friend on this earth you have.

Ne-yo has a song on his album "Year of the Gentleman," that makes you think about how crazy it is to sit around buggin' over something which is no longer in your control. The song title is, "So You Can Cry.*" Check out how the lyrics relate to getting over someone and moving on:

"So it's over, he's with someone else, and you know her

And you just can't get any lower

You sit in the dark alone,

And won't answer your phone…

*Written by Shaffer Smith and Reggie Perry

Well, I'm sorry…I won't attend your pity party

I would rather go have calamari,

And maybe a drink, and yes I think

You should come with me

Life is long…there will be pain, but life goes on

With everyday, a brand new song,

But if you rather stay at home

Let me do you a favor

I'll ask the sun to shine, away from you, today so you can cry…

If that's what you want alright

I'll ask the clouds to bring the rain to you, today so you can cry…

If that's what you want alright"

I know it is just a song, but there is something to be learned here from the delivery. Ne-yo is telling his friend, "Look…you can cry, and I'll help you out. Let me get the clouds for you, bring some rain and you can step your game up on your pity party but I am not staying. I am not down; it is time to move on." He is making light of the situation, but you have to be able to step back and do the same thing. Being heartbroken sucks but it sucks more to dwell in it. Would you recommend a friend wallow in self-pity? Nope! Pick it up, dust it off and keep it moving!

I have a friend who had this crazy experience. I am guessing there are more women out there who can attest to dealing with some variation of the experience I am about to share than would like to admit it. This is for you. This is a situation where this friend would have never, ever given this advice to someone else, but as I was telling her to move on, she was telling me she would do it in her own time and space. I respect this decision but as you read the situation, ask yourself if you were in this situation, how much time would you need?

We will call this friend Claudia. Claudia is a knockout. Babi girl is a tall, beautiful woman with all the right curves in all the right places. Claudia makes is a point to be even more of who she is when she is going out. Dinner, dancing, whatever the function may be, she has been the "life of the party," since I have known her. I love Claudia so much. She was such a great friend and there for me when I needed her, when I was working through issues of my own with different people in my life. Just as a side note, a definition of a friend should not be someone who is only there when they need you…it should always be a relationship of reciprocity. Always. The reciprocity may be different things to different parts and parties of the relationship. A relationship which is only giving on one end and taking on the other does not meet the criteria of a true friendship and it needs to be respected for what it is…an association of convenience. When building the friendship relationship, look for more true friends and work to weed out relationships of convenience.

Claudia had this crazy situation. She was really into this guy and wanted to date him, so she did her thing. The problem is, he had a girlfriend. There was constant drama within his relationship with the girlfriend but never really a move on his part to leave and cut the girlfriend loose completely; though there were no real strings attached (not married, no kids, etc.). Claudia was so in love with this dude. She might do her thing on the side every now and then, because she knew she was the chick on the side, but Claudia has the "gift" (the world would call it a gift, a Christian would call it a curse) to be able to distinguish sex from love. That was a blessing and a curse. It was a curse because Claudia could cut him out of her life for moments but she is still a lady with emotions and feelings, and she very much loved him. Therefore she could not cut this guy out of her life forever. This went on for several years…yes, that is not a typo, I said YEARS. At some point, Claudia was certain this dude was also adding some more toppings to his cake and had *another* girl on the side. Still, that was not enough to get him out of Claudia's life. Finally, after years of this crazy affair, he moved, and I believe the time away finally showed her he was not down for her like she thought he would be. Now, throughout this journey, I am begging Claudia to let him go. Nothing against him, I do not know him, he may be a great guy, though clearly misguided. She deserved better; a heck of a lot better! I do not think she ever believed he would marry her but I do think she convinced herself he would kind of take care of her, after the other chicks were gone and he could see she was really the "ride or die" chick. I brought up that phrase in an earlier chapter. Ladies, you have the game of being the strong supportive woman inverted in some way. The ride or die chick (strong, supportive woman who will stick with her man through thick and thin) should be the woman who has her man's back, because *he* has her back. Not because she is willing to show her unconditional love and loyalty no *matter* what. There is something which should definitely *matter*! He needs to show he is down in whatever way that means. It should mean a monogamous relationship. It should mean a ring on your finger. It should mean, bringing you home to his parents house to meet them, instead of him coming to your house, after he *just* left his girlfriend's house (What kinda nonsense? It gets me fired up just thinking about that—and yes, that happened in the previous story). Claudia has a child and this tenet has come up in the form of a question during our conversations when she was in this relationship. I even asked at the time if she had a daughter and the daughter were going through the same thing she was, what advice she would give her. She said something like and I paraphrase, "I would tell her to do whatever she thought was best." Claudia would tell her daughter to do whatever she thinks is best...I do not think she was lying. I also think she would be quick to point out, best is not playing second to anyone. Now, I ask you...would you recommend someone be the other woman in any relationship? Now take that advice and apply it to yourself. All the time, every time!

Finally, I have an example which is also relevant to this tenet. I have another friend, we will call her Rochelle. Rochelle has a man, who by her account, most guys cannot live up to his standards. He takes care of her, if she is with him, he has got the bill, or whatever she wants to buy at the mall. If I listened to her, he would be my inspiration as a man. There are a couple of problems, though. It seems he is compensating for something, because he has some deficiencies within the context of their relationship. Oh, they are not your little run of the mill, "forgets to fold laundry" type deficiencies, either. He cheated with another woman, multiple times. Finally and maybe worst of all, he will not commit. I guess it is because he has cheated with the same woman multiple times...and committing to Rochelle might mess that up. This is just a guess, though I could be mistaken (forgive the sarcasm).

Now, Rochelle is a very intelligent woman. We are not very close, I would not call her part of my inner circle but she shared this with me. This was such a no-brainer, I asked her, "If your daughter were doing this, would you advise her to keep doing it?" She said and I quote, "Oh, I would not advise anyone to do what I'm doing." She followed it up with, "you only live once." I assume her rationale was, you only live once, so you may as well take a chance on what you want or what you think you want. I am sure Rochelle knows the following, but I am going to say it anyway. If he could cheat on you and you could reconcile, then so be it. I assume everyone deserves the benefit of the doubt. When he went back and did it again, with the same woman, apparently, he had to have known he was going there again, because he did not get rid of her number or change his number to make sure she could not contact him. She wonders why he will not commit. He has his cake, icing, the candles, balloons and clowns, so why would he ever stop the party? The sad thing is, at some point, he probably will commit. He can have the benefits of being married and the benefits of an outside relationship, all at the same time. If you know a guy/girl is cheating as you go into a relationship (or get back in one) and it has a recurring theme…that may be a sign. The sign should read "Get da heck out! Now!" If he sells you on the fact he has changed, that is great. You want to believe him but no matter what he says, if he has done the same things over and over, what makes you think he will not continue? Ladies, sometimes emotion and feelings have to be *totally* removed from the equation and good ole common sense should come into play. No matter what he says, his pattern of behavior and actions say something different than what he is communicating in words. I hope Rochelle uses the good sense she was blessed with and makes the right decision. She actually already made it when she said, "I would not advise anyone to do what I'm doing," but she is determined to follow her heart…but how many times does he have to break it for her to get the picture? His word says the heart is deceitful above all things. If the Creator lives in you, use his Word to help your judgment, to advise both friends and yourself. Then follow your discernment. If you do not love yourself enough to listen to your own good judgment, you do not love yourself enough to get into a relationship.

Chapter Seven

TRYING TO PUT THE CART BEFORE THE HORSE

Ironically enough, I spoke about the narcotic that love is and how it can make you step outside of who you are in many ways. I think the euphoric feeling of love combined with the rush we get from pleasure and the need to feel loved leads us into the next topic. Also, from the conversations I have had around this topic, this seems to be the topic where men do not pick this up as quickly as women do. I can certainly say I did not. The things I write about here were totally foreign to me only a few years ago. This is a key component to a successful relationship. All of the chapters are important, but this one is very specific and it may be the most highly debated of the topics I write about.

As I was preparing to write this chapter, I was speaking with a friend about all the thoughts I had and the fact I had a lot to say about it. I was telling her how confident I was in my findings and how if she looked at what I was talking about in the people around her, she could see evidence of my findings. Eventually, I was able to convince her, my philosophy was a "rule" not an "exception." This is a debate, which I am sure many people will take me to task on (as my friend did), because this is a topic where I have found we have not thought the process through overall as a society.

I made plenty of mistakes growing up and my grandmother was there to remind me of what I did, right or wrong. She was the foundation and primary influence in my upbringing. I would not say she was soft spoken, but I would say when she was telling me the most important things, she would not say a lot. I chose to live with a woman, before considering marriage (before considering a promise ring for that matter), much too early in my life. I do not regret it; it is part of what has made me who I am today. My grandmother let me know very simply, I was trying to "put the cart before the horse." I am sure I had heard that phrase in other ways relating to life before, but this time it did not make much sense to me; as I now know it should have. Tenet number four is controversial, but I intend to alleviate some of that controversy in this chapter:

Tenet #4: Do Not Live With Someone Before Marriage

I am sure living together before marriage has worked for some people. I can only speak to my friends and acquaintances experiences which I am privy to. There may be more, but out of the people I know, there are two couples who lived together before marriage, who are currently in working marriages. I can think of eleven couples, at a quick glance, who have lived with someone (at least once, some many times) in relationships which did not end up working.

First of all, if you are living together, what is the goal? Is the goal to permanently cohabitate? Is the goal to get married? Is the goal to live together for a while, until you find a better situation? I would have to say, of those people I know who have lived together, the goal of the woman has *always* been to eventually be married. What tends to happen is when the couple moves in together, there is no communication on what the goal is. The woman seems to always believe this is a stepping stone to marriage. Some guys think this as well. I would say most of the time, the male philosophy tends to be different. Quite often, guys leave their intentions undefined and quite vague around this situation.

I cannot speak to every man's philosophy on living together, but this will account for a large portion of us out there. Most guys feel like if we can live with a woman and everything is working out the way we envision it should work; then we can *eventually* see ourselves married to them. I had the same philosophy but it is totally flawed. Stated another way, we feel like we are "practicing at marriage." We are finding out if we can live with her flaws, her good points and everything that goes with the woman we proclaim to the world we love so much. We are so "sprung," but yet we are so unsure about babi girl, we feel like we need a trial run to make sure this is going to be truly as great as we expect it to be.

This sounds like it makes some sense in theory, but in application, it is probably the most incorrect methodology of any we apply to our relationships. We want to practice like we are married, but in truth we *are* married, just without the piece of paper. We want to act like we are practicing the game, but in reality, we are playing the game and now we have, in effect, given each other too many outs. I know it sounds like I am talking about baseball but let me explain what I mean.

When we actually get married, those first three to five years are sometimes very difficult. Getting to know one another, tendencies, mood swings, things we may not have noticed when we were dating now seem to make a difference. Financially, it is often tough in the early stages of marriage. There are a lot of things to deal with which make the first few years challenging for the strongest of relationships. Someone along the line decided they would be a little smarter than the average bear and they would cohabitate first. They would try it out…see if it fits. The problem is when you try to live with someone, you are doing it without true commitment. "That is my boo, we have been down forever…I'm never going to leave her…we will get married one day." Yeah, right! I have heard this phrase rearranged and said many different ways and it is a lie (most of the time) no matter how it comes out. It carries about as much weight as Nixon saying he was not a crook, Clinton saying he did not have sexual relations with that woman or McGwire saying he was not on steroids.

As long as we can leave a relationship without consequences, then we are actually jeopardizing the relationship, more than growing it. Consequences, as it relates here, does not mean a lease to an apartment with both parties' name on it, one person moving all their stuff into another person's house or even a mortgage together. We can and will walk away from a financial or other responsibility if we feel pissed off enough to leave. Guys, we are the worst at this. You can walk away from all of those things I just stated very easily but you cannot walk away from a marriage nearly as easily. Divorce statistics are extremely high but in a marriage, you are much more apt to trying to make it work and working through issues than you would be when simply living together.

I came home one day when I was living with someone and found all of my clothes stacked up on the bed. I cannot remember what I did but if I had to guess it had something to do with my lack of discipline in my finances. It is a challenge of mine which impacted that particular relationship but although it was a challenge, had we been married, we would have worked through it…or at the very least made a much better attempt working through it. I did not leave that day; I calmly picked up my clothes and put them back in the closet, but the damage was done. We had practiced the game in our minds (but we were actually playing the beginning stages of the game in reality). She did not like the issues I had (she had some, too) but the point is since we were not one-hundred percent committed, it made it easy for her to decide to end our relationship. I also have a footnote to this experience. I had to learn the following lesson the hard way but let my moment of discontentment be your revelation. Guys, never, ever, ever, move into a woman's house. A woman who can do for herself realizes first and foremost, she does not *need* you. She may want you but she does not need you and she will never forget it…and in the worst moments, she will remind you in no uncertain terms. Even when she really wants to give you the benefit of the doubt, once she has had it with whatever the situation is, you may want to go ahead and get to stepping, because at that point the place is no longer "ours" is it "hers." I find guys are not like that nearly as much, if a woman moves in with them but women can be a little more possessive when their hearts are on the line. Therefore, to save you some drama, make it a point to not move into her house without being in covenant. I am trying to save you some embarrassment and drama when it is time to bounce. Never move to her spot...because when you start trippin', the nicest of women will remind you whose spot it is. Believe me on this also; it does not matter if you are paying every bill and doing every chore, it will be irrelevant once you have pissed her completely off. This is my public service announcement for the guys.

These situations rarely, if ever work and it seems they often do not end well. Let's look at a couple of examples.

One of my friends and I used to hang out at a local university around lunchtime from time to time. We were college age, so we would play spades, listen to music and do whatever college age kids did. He was living with a woman at the time. This may be the biggest understatement of my life, but she had a bit of a temper on her. One day, we go to the school, chill out, get some lunch and have a good time. I can remember she was upset when he left...he did not say much other than, "let's go." Cool, I did not have to hear her drama and we were out of there pretty quickly. We were on our way back from lunch and as we pull into his driveway, I ask, "Man, what is that on your front porch?" As we get closer, he is like, "what da...!" I never would have bet such a little woman could move so much stuff in an hour and a half. She put ALL of his stuff out on the sidewalk. All of it! Not one thing of his was left in the house. Of course, she still had to come outside and put on a little bit of a show, just in case he did not get the point. I helped him pick up his stuff and he moved in with me for a couple of weeks. The point is, they were not yet married and this did not help the situation. They did wind up getting married, but it did not work out. Guys like to believe we can reinvent the wheel, but we cannot. Marriage and the attributes which are a part of it; love, commitment, honor and trust are there for a reason. Do it the right way, with the right heart, right mind and right tools, and it will work for you.

I have an experience from another friend I want to share. I know a few people with similar experiences to the one I am about to describe, so unfortunately, it is much too common. I have a friend, we will refer to him as Charles. Charles has been dating a woman off and on for a long time, too many years to count, at least a decade. I do not doubt for a second they love one another. They have children and they take care of them together. The problem is they have lived together for so long, I am not sure what they are expecting to come out of what they have. There have been times where he was struggling and she would take care of him. There have been times where she needed his help and he took care of her. They had all of the moving parts of a marriage, but Charles did not want to commit to marriage because it was never "good enough." Again, here is a situation where living together was harmful and it helped to end their relationship. It is such a shame in this case, because they have a beautiful family and I believe they are good for each other; but they went about it the wrong way. Once you live together, you think you are practicing but after a while it becomes so routine, you simply are coasting along. You would like to see things get better but what many couples are missing is the fact that they are not fully enjoying the journey as they should, because they are not totally committed to what they are trying to accomplish together. Sometimes we get caught up in external things. We want to have a big house, a BMW and a Benz in the garage. We want to be able to have what we think we should have or even worse, what we think we need to have to keep up with our acquaintances. Life is about the journey. We want to believe it is about the pinnacle but it is really about how you get there. This experience is so much about who Charles and his girlfriend thought they were supposed to become, as opposed to about who they are. We have to realize, we must accept one another as we are and grow together. Often, we want to expect things to be a certain way once we live together or for our mate to change to conform to our standards and this is like some "probationary period" to do so. If you cannot love your woman or man for who they are and be willing to commit to them and accept them for that; then at least have the ability, (some might say the decency) to allow them to move on and be with someone who accepts them for who they are and how they impact someone's life.

Chapter Eight
ALL DAY, EVERY DAY

The last two tenets were very in-depth, which could weigh heavily on the mind and require a lot of thought. Just because something is a characteristic of a successful relationship, does not always mean it has to be complicated. I believe sometimes we need to use the most basic thought processes when thinking about how to keep our relationships moving in the direction we want them to go. I can remember dating a young lady when I was very young. We had several arguments and "falling outs" so to speak. Long after the relationship was over and we had both moved on, she told me something I never forgot. She said, "You would come back to apologize and make up, but you would always come empty-handed." Of course, we all have different perspectives on gifts. During this relationship, my methodology was whether I am making up or just being the best significant other I can be, I do not want anyone to feel like I am trying to buy their companionship or love. Therefore, when we had problems, if I was trying to make up to her, I would not bring a gift. She felt the opposite. She felt I needed to bring a token of my appreciation to show her I was thinking about her if we were going to begin to make this work. I should have communicated with her to find out how to show her my affection, especially in situations where she was angry, frustrated or hurt by my actions or a situation.

I feel a lot of us miss the mark when it comes to showing how we feel for each other. Whether we are dating or married, we seem to find it very easy to find the negative in one another. To make matters worse, we have many other factors influencing how we interact with one another. Children, careers, school, in-laws, religious beliefs, political views, financial situations, friends and so many other things influence how we treat each other on a day to day basis. Life happens and it becomes so easy to forget why we got together in the first place. This tenet is not as complicated as some but it requires sincerity and an ability to remember you are in this together because you truly love this person:

Tenet #5: Show Appreciation

When our children make mistakes, it is so easy to come down on them. Sometimes, you do not give them proper appreciation for the twenty things they do right, before they do the two consecutive things wrong. The same things happen at work. Many employees feel under-appreciated. Those feelings can transfer to life at home. If you feel your employer does not appreciate what you do, you go home and you are not happy. Often, pay is an irrelevant issue; you simply want to be appreciated for the commitment you make to the corporation. I believe this issue speaks to some of the reason we do not appreciate one another in relationships as we should. If we were appreciated all day, every day, we would be reminded what it is like to appreciate and it would transfer to life at home. Fortunately, we are all adults and we do not have to wait for our job to condition us to do the smart, considerate thing; we can train ourselves.

We have all done or seen someone do something for their mate "just because." I think people who say they do not like surprises are even a bit taken back by a nice bouquet of flowers or their favorite cologne. If you are not used to doing things for your mate "just because," take note…this is a great opportunity for you and your relationship. It almost goes without saying the fact of thinking of your mate (speaking to both men and women) without it being a holiday or birthday is something you want to do. Showing appreciation does not always have to be a bouquet of flowers. Guys, remember that ladies are wired differently than we are. This may be so small to some of us fellas, we cannot even fathom how this makes it into a book…but I am about to give you an example of appreciation which will blow your mind.

One of my friends went on a short trip. She put her cell phone down and I think she may have been driving for a few hours. Her man put her phone on the charger for her, simply because the phone was sitting where he happened to see the battery was dying. That is all he did. I bet she has told this story to me three or four times, and she breaks into an uncontrollable smile each time. That may be the simplest expression of appreciation someone could show for another person, but it made her day…maybe her week! The fact he paid enough attention to notice her phone was down and then made the effort to put it on the charger...that was so incredibly thoughtful to her. Guys please do not run around looking for phones to put on chargers…this is not the point. It may not do anything for another woman, but for this lady, she was simply impressed at the detail of her man's thoughtfulness.

Women think men are sometimes oblivious to their wants and desires. We are not oblivious; we have not been taught how to notice what women really want. Guys, understand that women want you to pay attention to everything, but especially the little things. Pay attention to the details of her life. I have dated women who will only wear one perfume. Dig this…if your woman only wears one brand of perfume…you need to know what that perfume is called and at some point, you need to get her the package with the soap, body spray and all of the other accessories which go with that perfume. If your lady has a favorite designer, know who the designer is and consider that designer when picking something out for her. Learn what she likes and does not like as far as style. Does she wear turtlenecks? Is she into sundresses? I know we all are not fashionistas but honestly, the less of a fashion guru you are; the more she will appreciate it when you bring home something she might actually wear.

Ladies, you have to appreciate the men as well. I once had a girl send me a dozen roses to my job, while she was on the other side of the country. They had to be the largest, prettiest roses I have ever seen, before or since. I am not all into roses, so I gave one to each woman I worked with. The thought that my girl put into sending me roses was really nice, because she knew it was something I would never expect. Not only did I appreciate it but I was able to give them to others to appreciate as well; which also made me happy. He may not be able to get with the flowers, but consider cards, emails and maybe even a romantic text message during the middle of the day…anything to let him know you are thinking about him.

Guys, you would be surprised how many women will be willing to help a man out in the lingerie section (I guess it is all a lingerie section) at Victoria's Secret. As a matter of fact, the more lost you look, the more help you will get. For those of us who are not married, obviously we do not want to go over the top with lingerie, but even though you will not be "enjoying it" so to speak, she will, and she will appreciate the fact you thought about her.

Appreciation goes farther than buying one another things. Remember the story about me cutting the grass and my girl offering me water. It was a nice gesture, but honestly, she was showing her appreciation for what I was doing for her. She could have been asleep or chillin reading a book like this one, but she was showing me love, when she did not have to. That is the ultimate point. I can remember the same woman was out of town once, and brought me back a necklace and bracelet. I would have never thought I would wear either of them. She bought one for each of us and we wore them from time to time. Interestingly enough, the necklace came up missing when we broke up (suspect), but I still have the bracelet and it reminds me of fond memories and most of all, it reminds me of her appreciation. She did not have to do that for me, but she took the time to show her appreciation. Show your mate love in some way, shape, form or fashion, even though it is not required at the time.

If you know your lady is from the country, but now you live in New York City, take her horseback riding one weekend, for the nostalgia of it. Maybe take her camping or even fishing. Get to know her intricacies, study them and cater to them. When you show appreciation, it is all about your mate. Guys sometimes lose this in translation. We mean well but we have been known to bring home a vacuum cleaner or new set of pots and pans as a present. If she is cooking like Chef Emeril Lagasse, maybe you try the pots and pans as a gift. If not, most likely the next sound you hear will be "Bam!" That will not be your boo adding an ingredient to a dish like Chef Emeril, that will be the sound of the pot ringing against your temple. Pots and Pans--accept them as wedding gifts, do not offer them as a present to your mate. Never buy gifts to fill a need—unless that need coincides with a desire of hers.

I can remember being with the woman I spoke of earlier in this chapter (who wanted me to bring gifts as a token) and she enjoyed the way I treated her. We will call her Nikki. I remember one day, Nikki took me out with her and her girlfriends. As her girlfriends each dogged their man, I just knew Nikki was going to put me on blast and dog me as well, regardless if I was sitting there or not. I thought I did a better-than-average job showing my appreciation for Nikki, but this was a man-hating session, I could not imagine getting out of this unscathed. When Nikki talked about me, she said not only do I do what I am supposed to do, but I go above and beyond when it comes to how I treat her. I was pleasantly surprised and a little shocked! Obviously, how I treated her overall is more than simple appreciation, but it played a significant role. Guys, we have all heard the man-hating conversations, "he's no good," "he doesn't do this" "he can't make me (sexual innuendo)..." Yes, ladies we have heard them, too. The challenge I am making for the guys is to pay attention to detail. As a matter of fact, pay attention to the most minute details. Even when we get it wrong sometimes, showing the effort will pay off in the long run toward building a strong relationship—and avoiding being a topic of discussion in a man-bashing session.

Finally, I have a friend who had the appreciation part of the equation down pretty well. Lingerie, jewelry, trips, shopping…just about whatever you can name, he has done it for his lady. My friend is not ballin (urbandictionary.com defines 'ballin' as living in affluence/wealth). He does not have a lot of money. He is smart with his money and he plans ahead. He pays attention to detail and finds out what she likes and does not like. He does not always get it perfect, but his effort is always on point, so even if he messes up, he gets a pass because his lady could see how hard he was trying to make her happy and show how much he appreciates her. Obviously, this is not as dramatic or intriguing a story as opposed to someone who is not doing what they are supposed to do. The difference is he is not sleeping on the sofa or in the dog house. It is worth spending some time, thought and effort to stay out of the dog house.

Here is the chance to show love in its verb form at its best. Pay attention to detail, all day, every day. Find out your mate's likes and dislikes. Think outside the box. Remember, you do not always have to pay for something to show you appreciation. Whatever you decide to plan, do not do it out of a feeling of obligation; do it out of a spirit of love. These small things will make your mate think of you often, because they know how much you appreciate them—which in turn makes them appreciate you.

Chapter Nine
YOU ARE NOT ALONE

We all have them. You have to learn to accept them from the beginning of the relationship. They are what make us who we are. You have to love them (to an extent) as much as you love the other characteristics in your mate. They can be confusing at times; almost not exactly what they seem to be. At other times, "they are who we thought they were!" They are not leaving. They are not getting better. You and I both will always have them. Yes, they absolutely suck. Yes, they can make you think of divorce and different types of pre-meditated homicide. They can also be kinda sexy in a compromising moment (in case any married folks are reading this). Completely confused yet? You will not be for long.

To accept someone is to love them unconditionally. The definition of unconditionally is "not limited by conditions." You say you love someone unconditionally, but the moment that *thing* pops up about them that you hate, that you despise; you are ready to reconsider. If you want to enter into a relationship with someone, you must consider the good traits and bad traits they have. You must be willing to work with all that person is, as you meet them today…not all that you expect they will be tomorrow. This tenet is a tough pill to swallow for some, even myself in the past, but you have to figure out how to do it to have a healthy relationship:

Tenet #6: Decide if You Can Live with the Flaws of Your Mate

Again, this is not an easy topic, but a necessary one. You want to deal with people on an intimate level, a spiritual level but you are not sure if you can get past that sound they make with their teeth. This is an example but it is important to note the concept. We all have flaws. We all have imperfections. I suppose if they were physical traits we could call them "pimples" or "blotches." Understand from the beginning, most, if not all of these things are never going to change in your mate. You have certain characteristics that will bother some people but will be irrelevant or cute to others. Some people talk too much, some not enough; some are flashy, some are too shy; some people are really mean, some are extraordinarily nice; some are a little dingy, some seem to live in the world of Logic like Mr. Spock. Some people seem to (or believe they) know everything, some people clearly know nothing; some people are much too bourgeois, some people are way too ghetto; some people worry all the time, some people seem to "give a rat's tail." Finally, some people are very condescending, and some people are ridiculously timid; some people are too quick to love and some people are too slow to accept love.

All of these traits are conditions of who we are. Many of

these things will never change within us. Some things, we do grow out of; maybe a few things change over time. Maturity in our spirit and maturity as a human being will help with some of these challenges. Some of these traits can be tempered but still they are a part of us and they are not leaving.

When you are making the decision about your mate as you are getting to know your mate, realize they are most likely not going to change. If you are taking this person as a mate and not accepting them for who they are, you are doing yourself and them a disservice. You cannot expect anyone to make drastic or even what may be, in your mind, subtle changes to characteristics which are a part of who they are. I mentioned some of these things earlier in the book. Can we change putting the top on the toothpaste, or folding the laundry? Yes, I think we should be able to make changes in the things we do, but not necessarily in who we are. I talked about my friend who had a trait I could not deal with. She still had some feeling of resentment for how she was treated in a past relationship. It is understandable, especially from her perspective. I should not have asked her to change how she felt; I should have let her work through it. Eventually, I tried to give her time to work through it but her lack of closure in some issues came to light in ways that were a deal-breaker for me. It did not change the fact I loved her. It did not change the fact she is a great woman, deserving of a great man. What I finally did, for both of us, is something we would have been forced to do later and probably much more unpleasantly. I had to let go. If you cannot live with a trait, you cannot continue forward with that person. If the trait or flaw in your mind is bigger than the relationship; you have to let it go. No one is winning; no one is getting better or growing. The good times are overshadowed by the bad. Learn yourself enough to know what you can and cannot live with. Not only do you deserve it but the person you are with deserves someone who knows they are completely committed to every portion of you…not just the good parts of you.

The largest problems I see with the experiences around me are not whether or not we accept the flaws. The problem is we expect the person to change the way we want them to, after we "make it official." I think many of us believe we can see the potential and the good in someone, and how they make our lives better in many instances…except for one or two "little" things. You feel you can fix those things and once again, "Bam," it's all good. It is not all good, because knowing the attributes you can and cannot deal with is only the beginning. You also must know how to accept those attributes which are challenging and how to deal with them. Sometimes, compromise on things is not an option. For example, if you are dating a strong willed person and this is a challenge you are willing to accept, you must accept you will have to acquiesce sometimes to their stubbornness. You have to figure out as you go along how to pick and choose battles you are willing to fight along the lines of dealing with the flawed characteristic of your mate. Take the time to figure out what really bothers you about them and talk to them about it. Communicate how you feel. Let them know you understand they are not going to change and you do not expect them to; but also help them understand it is not the most becoming characteristic in their personality. Get them to listen to how you really feel about it, and therefore when they are exhibiting this characteristic, they are conscious of it, at least, and take your feelings into consideration. Again, you are not asking them to change and you should not. What you are asking is they are considerate of your feelings when you are working through your challenges. Communication is crucial when dealing with oppositional forces within relationships. Talk through things and make it a point to work through things together. Relationship challenges are hurdles which when worked through *together* will almost always make the relationship come out stronger on the other side.

I am no different than anyone else. I have my issues. I have a sarcastic attitude and I am often inclined to be nonchalant. Summed up, I seem to always have a comment which is many times unnecessary and on top of that, I could care less what you think about it. I often wish I could change it. I have very sensitive friends who think I am being inconsiderate and insensitive of their feelings when I talk to them. In my mind, I am being the exact opposite. I feel I am being the voice of reason; the voice of common sense when others around them are sugar-coating everything. Truth be told, I can be abrasive and tactless, when I could definitely get the same point across with sensitivity and a compassionate attitude. I do not intend to be this way; it is the way I am made. It is part of who I am; it is a part of my DNA. Those that are around me, a part of my inner circle must learn and accept this about me. I have learned this about myself enough to know who I am. Therefore I can communicate to my friends that I do what I do out of love and not with a condescending or demeaning attitude but with a straight-forward, "keep it real the only way I know how" attitude. I bring up a couple of my character flaws to make the point; we all have them. More importantly, we need to learn and be aware of them. If we can temper them, that is even better. Change is always good and you should change yourself for the better whenever you can. Be that as it may, you cannot change every part of who you are and the sooner we understand ourselves and our mates; the sooner we work through challenges together to build productive, successful relationships.

I want to speak a bit more about change and how it relates to how we feel about our flaws. Change will come from individual growth, but you may not be able to see the change you want or are hoping for in your mate; so understand you may never see the change you expect. Therefore, you cannot count on something which is most likely not going to happen. Your heart will deceive on this point when blinded by the desire to be with someone. Trust your intellect to make thoughtful decisions, and while we should to some extent "follow our heart," also use your mind to keep your heart in check. Especially with realizing we cannot change others. Here is an example where I decided, I could not change someone, but I could live with the "flawed" characteristic. I dated a woman who had the capability not to speak to me for hours and on occasion, days at a time. I do not like to go to sleep upset, so this was extremely tough for me. I needed to decide if it was a deal breaker for me. It was tough for me, but I decided I could work through it. You have to know what you really can and cannot deal with to make a relationship productive. I know a young lady who is dating a guy who has a job, but he is not really making any money, though he is quite capable of making a lot of money if he followed another career path. She loves him enough to believe in him and be accepting of his decision. Again, here is a challenge which they are working through together and it is not a deal breaker. She cannot change him, it will not happen through "evolution"; he made a decision to do what he does career-wise and they are accepting it. Working together is really about accepting each other, not throwing things in each other's face and moving forward together; even through the imperfections. Finally, I have another friend; we will call her "Gloria." Gloria has a man who lives out of town, but he is trying to date her and get to know her better. He continually calls and sends text messages, trying to set up a time to get together with Gloria. The problem is, months have passed, and the guy has done a great job of playing Gloria off, and now she is somewhat suspicious of him. He is never available to come and see her, and when she offers to come and see him it does not work for him. To her, there is something obviously blocking every opportunity they have to get together, though he continually calls. She feels he is lying about his current situation at home and his actions have brought him to a point where he has created a deal-breaker with Gloria. He talks about seeing her, but only on his terms and even when those opportunities arise, he is not around. Gloria feels he is hiding something and his actions have eliminated any chance he had of a relationship with her. She cannot and is not trying to change him. Gloria is simply moving forward toward another opportunity; not dwelling on something which never took shape.

I like to have a little fun, especially with my sports analogies, so here is a great example of a flaw in a relationship, I could not live with—nor should the good people of Detroit be forced to:

I love the city of Detroit. Would I bet one dollar that the Lions are going to win the Superbowl? Heck to the no! I respect the Detroit Lions franchise, but history tells me they have a critical flaw, when compared to the rest of the league when it comes to winning and especially, winning super bowls. The flaw of not building the best team (even with a talented Barry Sanders, for example), is something as a fan, I cannot live with. In comparison, troubled hedge fund broker (or liar…however you want to phrase it) Bernie Madoff has made a lot more people happy than the Detroit Lions. There was a return on your investment from Madoff Investment Securities for twenty-nine years-and a very high return-between 20% and 30% return, before its collapse in late 2008. The Lions have won only two playoff games in the super bowl era. The ROI on the Lions from a fan's perspective has to be terrible for the past thirty years. Something more like the ROI on GM over the past decade. Maybe the Lions can get bailout money…it still would not help. They have a trait for building talented, yet under-achieving, non-cohesive teams. It is a trait if I lived in the city of Detroit, I could not live with as a fan. I would have to decide I could not live with their flaws and send them packing…Go Cowboys!

As you grow together, you will see relatively quickly what traits about your mate you can and cannot live with. The toughest part about the entire process of thinking about their flaws (and yours) is not acknowledging them, but accepting you cannot live with something and letting it go. You will save yourself and them a lot of pain. Much like the rest of the tenets of a successful relationship, follow this tenet and you will be closer to making your current relationship successful or finding the person you are destined to be with. Be honest with yourself and your mate, and even though it may be a tough decision, success will follow a *correct* decision.

Chapter Ten
WHAT SHOULD I WEAR

When you are dating someone and you enjoy their company; you work hard to make sure they see you in the best light. For example, when a date comes over, you try to make sure the house is clean. When you go out, you like to be fresh and dressed appropriately for whatever the event is you two are attending. You and your representative I spoke of earlier are doing your best to put your best foot forward so this person will reciprocate. When you like someone, you want them to like you as well. It is only natural for each of us to want the person in our lives at that moment to be impressed with us and we want to be impressed with them. It is never a matter of being someone you are not or putting up a front of someone you are incapable of being. You are trying to showcase who you are at your best and you hope to see the same; so you may give the same respect, admiration, and hopefully, attraction to one another.

Dating is fun and it should be fun and anyone who disputes this has not done it properly. Finding who to date can sometimes be a daunting task, to say the least. Some of you have a knack for knowing exactly who floats your boat. Some of you have a knack for being attracted to the exact opposite of the person you believe you need in your life. Regardless, once you find someone you want to spend time with, dating this person should be a very enjoyable experience. Here is how it will go…a template of sorts. This is not necessarily for the first date, but as long as the representative is around, you can bet this template or some slight variation is in use. You talk on the phone or email/text for hours to get to know one another. Next, you decide where you want to go. You decide on time, place, where to meet, who is driving, etc. You pick out a great outfit just for that occasion, hit the shower, put on your favorite fragrance and now you are ready. You meet for dinner, a movie, salsa dancing, whatever the event is for the evening and you enjoy your time together. During the first three to six dates, the dates end with a separation as you have met somewhere or someone is dropping someone off. A nice hug or kiss is to follow. Then, as you ramp it up, you start to have dates at one another's homes in addition to the normal going out on the town. Someone is cooking for the other person or you may spend the night in, watching a movie. You take a walk around the neighborhood, or a nearby park. The point is, you are becoming more intimate (not talking sexually here) and comfortable with one another. The closer the relationship becomes, the more comfortable you become with each other. At some point a day will come when the representative leaves and through a challenge, disagreement, or argument, you two realize how close you have become and now you are being yourself.

This is normal, and a part of every relationship. The problem is, once we start to get comfortable, we forget the things we enjoyed doing together and forget what it was like to take walks in the park, stay up all night talking on the phone, going to dinner, going out dancing, playing spades with our friends, etc. You can easily let this slip away if you do not make a concerted effort for it not to happen. This brings me to the seventh tenet:

Tenet #7: Continue to Date Throughout the Relationship

I am sure everyone goes into relationships with the intention of following this tenet. No one thinks they will ever stop wanting to Salsa (for example). The fact is, they *will not* stop wanting to Salsa, but life and several other things in their environment will make it easy to forget about the things they enjoy doing together. I speak in another chapter about showing appreciation. A great way for you to show appreciation is to take the person who is the chef in the relationship out to a very nice dinner as often as possible. Show them you appreciate what they do. Now it is time for someone to cook a great meal for them, the way they cook for you. When we take moments to get away from the world and spend time with one another as often as possible, it makes the world seem like a more endearing place to be. Would you rather be the subject at work the next day of a conversation which starts off, "Girl, I can't believe he did not like what I cooked last night! That ungrateful, selfish…I worked all night on that recipe! Since he thinks I can't cook, he can cook Ramen tonight! He can add whatever seasoning he likes, with his pitiful…" You know where I am going with this hypothetical statement. Option B would sound more like this, "Girl, let me tell you what my man did for me last night. He took me to this new spot called Bricktops..it was sooooo good. He was so romantic. He had flowers waiting for me when he got there…then he ordered my dinner for me. It sends a chill down my spine just thinking about it." I would much rather hear reference to me as the subject of option B, easily. Guys, I have been around when these conversations take place. They definitely take place and you can get put on blast or you can be the man all of your woman's friends are hatin' on, because they cannot have you.

One of my friends is really good at treating his woman to different types of dates. I think they have probably been to every nice restaurant in our city. They have been on short excursions with other couples to resort cities. While they are away, they see the city together. They try different restaurants and nightclubs. They make it a point to still have quality time and date one another just like they did when their relationship started several years ago. They never let each other forget how they enjoy each other's company. The trials and problems in the world make it easy to forget how much we have fun together if we do not pay attention to making sure we are dating our mates.

This is one of my favorite tenets. I want to do new things together. I want to walk a nature trail or go shopping for the latest Prada bag for my boo (did I really say that? Hmmm…may have to think about that one). I remember I took a woman to an Indy Car Race. I like racing, so I was all about it, but I did not think for a moment she would like it. She loved it! We had so much fun. I do not know if she will ever go back to see a race. I am sure we will always remember that day as a day we shared a lot of fun together, although initially, we were both unsure how it would turn out. That was a very cool date and it is sometimes the dates which are outside the box that create the most memorable moments.

You know, if I ever have the bank account to afford it, I would like to be able to do a "soap opera" type date for my woman. I would like to fly my lady to Paris on a whim for dinner on the French Riviera. I would love to take her shopping on Fifth Avenue; give her my black American Express card and tell her the world is her oyster. I would also like for her to hit a powerball ticket and to take me to Monaco for dinner. Point being, I know we all want to do great things for our mates. Sometimes those things are expensive and out of reach. Do not let what you cannot do impact what you can do. Maybe you cannot take her shopping, but you know she loves to read. You can take her to the bookstore or library and spend some time there together. Like most of us, the French Riviera may be out of the budget right now but possibly you could do a spa day for both of you, which would be a date she would likely always remember—because she did it with you. I know he wants season tickets and you would love to buy them, but you do not have the money. What you could do instead is take him to the best sports bar in town and take care of everything. Be there with him and be supportive. Even though he knows you are not really a sports fan, he will be very appreciative, because you wanted to take him on a date to do something he loves to do.

Guys, this is an important tenet for us not to let get away.

We have to make a point to put forth the effort to date our ladies, always. I know someone who never goes out on a date. I will call her Dorinda. Dorinda does so much for her man and has ever since I have known them. I would be hard pressed to tell you the last time they went out together. They have had problems, and finally decided to go their separate ways. When they were together, Dorinda was the bread-winner for much of the time and domestic engineer. The travesty of the matter is, there is no doubt in my mind they would still be together if her man would have shown appreciation and continued to date her. Sometimes, you know people are not meant to be together. I never got that vibe from these two, but I do know this: Once Dorinda moved on from this relationship, she gets dates at this point, from others who want to give her attention. This is a story where had Dorinda's man chose to continue dating her, he would still be with her now.

Remember, what you put into the relationship is what you will get out of it. Take the time to enjoy your mate away from the house, the bills and the nine to five. Make it a point to see your mate in an environment where the ambiance enhances who they are. If she is an intimate woman who likes to be sexy, take her shopping at Victoria's, or if she likes nature, take her camping or something similar. Both of these women's smiles will light up like a Christmas tree when they hear what you are doing for a date with them. Keep your mate happy, you both deserve it and your mate will love you for it.

Chapter Eleven

THINK ABOUT WHERE YOU WANT TO ARRIVE

This is a tenet society seems to neglect having dialogue and discussion about. It is as important as any of the topics I have discussed. All of the nine tenets work in harmony to create a successful relationship. This does not mean if you follow all nine tenets to the letter every moment, you will have a life without bumps, doubts and turmoil…you will. Again, I do not guarantee many things, but those things, I can guarantee. There will be challenges and in relationships, we must face them together. Of course there are times we need to face some things alone. In most instances, once we are in a relationship, we share the challenges and we share the successes. Without a doubt, we must learn to remain individuals but acknowledge the ups and downs of life together.

Many times within the context of our relationship, we lose sight of what we want to do as a unit. You have so many things to do over the course of a given time period, it is easy to lose sight of where you want to go and what you would like to accomplish. I have found through my experiences our commonalities make it easy to relate to each other and our differences make us intriguing. It is our ability to want to accomplish things in life together, which enables our cohesiveness in a relationship. Whether the relationship is marriage, dating or the infant stages of getting to know one another…there is always a common goal, a desired outcome of where you want the relationship to go. You may refer to it as the "next step" or the "next level." This is a way of saying you have an accomplishment you want to achieve within the context of the relationship. It might be defining the relationship, it may be defining if you (as a man) are carrying *her* new last name or it may be defining if you as a couple want to move to France and open a restaurant, or whatever other great thing you may want to do together.

Should we expect any relationship to be successful, we have to expect growth both individually and as a couple. Sometimes we can be so caught up in ourselves, the kids, work, whatever the mitigating factor is, it can totally inhibit what we are actually trying to do. Tenet number eight is not spoken about enough and it is highly underrated. Take heed when I tell you:

Tenet #8: Concentrate on Growing Together

When you enter a relationship, you and your partner need to have the idea of how you are going to grow together in mind. If you are not on the same page on this topic with your mate, you are definitely in for problems. You have to look into the future and make decisions. You have to let your ambitions, your dreams and your passions, coincide to formulate a plan of how you want to grow together to accomplish what you want to achieve. For example, if one of you wants to finish your education and the other can help to make it happen and that works for your relationship, go for it! What needs to be addressed from the beginning is once one person has taken the leap of faith to help accomplish their mate's dreams, then the mate needs to reciprocate and help to accomplish the other person's dreams. Relationships have a certain amount of give and take. When you commit to growing together, sometimes there will be that give and take, but you will enjoy the journey and be rewarded with the spoils if you stay focused and grow *together*.

I have friends which I believe have absolutely no idea how to think in terms of growing together. Here is an example: We will call my friend "Tasha." Tasha has been dating this guy on and off (mostly on) for about 10 years. They have a child together and neither of them is going anywhere. They will be together for the duration of their lives. They do not want anyone else, they are not looking anywhere else. They are committed without the institute of marriage. This relationship astonishes me. She is frustrated with him from time to time and he gets frustrated with her. It is as though they expect perfection from one another and anything short of perfection is good enough for them to stay together as a couple, but not good enough to be married, be a cohesive family and grow together. I believe she thinks an actor from the series "Soul Food" is planning to come and sweep her out of this mess, and he thinks some supermodels are going to drive down their street someday and take him away from this frustration. Here is a news flash—it ain't gonna happen! The part that completely loses me is since they are both committed, (even though I think they would probably consider other options if the supermodels/actors came knocking) they will not even consider getting married. They live together, so that is a problem, but even more than that, they are a living example of what not growing together will do to a couple. Tasha has been with this man for a decade. They are somewhat on the same page but not with the same direction. They are so afraid if they get married they are stuck with one another, they have no intention of getting married. I relate to their relationship this way-technically, they are on the same page...one is on page ten of Home and Garden and the other is on page ten of Playboy. They could not have more different agendas if they were Rush Limbaugh and President Obama.

The previous situation occurs in some form all too often. Tasha and her man think marriage will make them end up stuck together. In reality, they already are. They have made a subconscious decision that they are comfortable and they do not want to change. They do not get any of the benefits of enjoying marriage and growing together. The situation has made itself conducive to growing apart or coasting along at best, but not growing together. The way their relationship has been built, everything has become a constant wave of chores which no one really looks forward to doing. If the relationship was built with the intent of growing together (and they stopped waiting on the supermodels/actors) they would find out they have a lot to offer and enjoy about one another. This couple only sees the negative of a relationship, sharing bills, raising a child, struggling to make ends meet. Nothing about their relationship is very fun. They spend little quality time together and they have a very predictable routine with no goals to achieve. They are simply living life with no specific purpose. No one deserves that, individually, or in a relationship.

Several years ago, I remember hearing a line in a rap song from a female rapper who said, "Ambition makes me horny." That may be a little too much information for some of us, but in reality there is some truth to it. Women want men who aspire to do something with their lives. You do not have to want to run a Fortune 500 company, but you want to show you have your sights set on growing as a man. Women, even the strongest of women, want men to be the head of the household. That does not mean running the household like boot camp, or being over-protective of everyone in the house. Something it does consist of is being a leader in directing where you want the family to grow to. A man in a leadership role needs to be able to defer to a woman's dream or ambition, if that is the most appropriate move for the family. Men need to have the ability to make a decision to foster growth within the family. If that means moving because the wife has a better opportunity in another state and it will help the family get closer to the things the family wants to accomplish, the man needs to have the leadership quality to make the decision to do what is best for the family. Guys, here is an important point: The *strongest* woman will look to her man for guidance. You do not have to be overbearing or condescending about it. Simply reiterate in your actions and words what is best for the family. Decide together where you want to grow to as a family. Men, make decisions to continue toward that growth and you will see your family thrive the way you expect it to. It may not be easy, it may not even be fun for everyone, but if you know it is best, make the decision and stick to it. Growth is about making choices, knowing full well some of those choices will be incorrect. Leadership is understanding when to make changes and redirecting steps in your life and your relationship. Ladies, every choice your man makes will not be perfect. Do not be so tough on him for making a wrong choice. Be supportive. Sometimes we have to make tough choices and live with the results. The sign of a healthy, successful relationship is not dwelling on whether you made a good or bad decision, it is how you respond accordingly to the decision you made. You will constantly learn and grow. Accept it, learn from your decisions and grow together.

I had to learn this tenet through experience and I hope I convey the message of concentrating on growing together to you as adamantly and frankly as I can. When I dated the love of my life at the time, she would talk about "what if" we did not already have children and we could pursue our dreams with uninhibited freedom. I am such a dreamer and so persistent and determined, I never bought into it. I felt like "why not?" Why did I have to change my dreams and ambitions? People do what I aspired to do every day and they had families and children to support; why did I have to change my agenda? My problem was the thoughts I was having about this issue were irrelevant to the situation. Her mind was made up; she was not about to consider moving to another state to pursue her dreams. She had decided her agenda was to raise her children the best she could right where she was and give them the life they deserved. I have no problem with that...but now I realize although I want that for my children as well, I still want to pursue my dreams.

Whether I see the dream come to fruition or not is almost irrelevant to the journey of trying to get there. I wanted to experience this journey with my mate. Had we been on the same page, things may have turned out better for our relationship but the truth of the matter is, it is best we realized we were not on the same page before we went to another level. There was no way we could grow together with different agendas. If we would have continued, it would have made the inevitable end of the relationship more difficult.

Growing together is not as difficult as we make it out to be. You need to determine what you want out of life and how to get there. This goes for every facet of life: spiritually, physically, financially and career-wise. It is good to create a plan and decide to how accomplish our desires. You also have to be flexible enough to know components of the plan will change from time to time and be willing to work with that. Marriage and relationships will always be comprised of moving parts. You have to know how to accept the ambiguity and embrace the change while continuing to grow together.

I have a situation I want to close this chapter with. I have a friend in the industry I once aspired to work in. He is married with a child. He has worked in this industry for some time. It can be very demanding, but rewarding at the same time. His wife also works in the same industry. They have different jobs at different levels but they can still relate to one another. My friend loves his wife very much. They do not have a perfect relationship, no one does. What they do have is a very committed relationship. A relationship where he tells me he does not allow temptation to ever be a possibility for him in an industry where temptation is abundant. He loves and cares for his child. He takes the opportunity (though he is extremely busy), to take trips and spend quality time with his family. He makes sure to reiterate the point of having spiritual growth with his family. He creates opportunities for his family to grow together and he has done so since the beginning of his relationship. The takeaway here is he *concentrates* on his family growing together. This is something at every point of a relationship we all need to do.

Chapter Twelve
THE BOTTOM LINE

Up to this point, we have covered eight important topics directed toward strengthening the health and well being of a relationship. It is difficult for me to tell you one tenet is more important than the others. I think they all have the utmost importance in building a successful relationship. How important is communication within the context of a successful relationship? How about appreciating one another? Understanding you must work together to build a strong relationship is a massive component to being successful. Realizing that living together before marriage is counter-productive could change countless lives. Being aware of the things you cannot live with would save a lot of pain and suffering people go through daily. Knowing that your advice and first instincts are just as good for you as they are for others (if not better) is key to making good choices. Doing things together (such as dating) just as you would from the beginning of the relationship could be the difference in adding years and possibly a lifetime to a relationship. Growing together will make one detrimental characteristic of any relationship impossible…growing apart.

All of these tenets are instrumental in keeping a relationship healthy and making it successful. That being said, this is the tenet you must work on every second of every day. This is the bottom line, the beginning and end to building a successful relationship. If you had to pick only one tenet to take away from this book...they are all important, but take this one with you always:

Tenet #9: Love, Honor and Respect

I hate to generalize, but if I was a betting man, I would be willing to wager there are some men who think I have just basically accused them of blatant stupidity. I am sure they are thinking, "Who would not know to do this?!" I am positive there are some right now who are thinking, "Duh, didn't I say this in my vows..." or something like, "Doesn't that go without saying?!" or maybe, "Tell me something I didn't know!" I grant you, this thought is not something new. The challenge you have is many of you do not do it! Remember, Love is a verb, disguised as a noun. Honor and Respect are verbs which are cleverly disguised as well.

First of all, to Love, Honor and Respect your mate is a privilege in and of itself. This person could have chosen anyone to have a relationship with or to marry. They are choosing of their own free will to be with you! You are privileged to have that opportunity. Do not take it for granted. Live in the moment and understand your opportunity to show this person these characteristics may be something they have never seen or experienced before. You may be the first person to show them what it is like to be cared for the way someone should in a relationship. Never take the opportunity to do these things for granted. Always respect the place where you are in your life and respect the place where you stand in another person's life by loving them accordingly.

Love is a verb. Do things for one another out of love. Ladies, if he needs silence for an hour just to read, then ask the kids to stay away from Dad for a while and give him some space. Guys, when you can see she is stressed or something is bothering her and there is no solution (as we like to fix everything), take her hand and tell her you are going to pray with her and for her. Whether you are a pastor or someone who never prays aloud or in public, showing your thoughtfulness for her to her Creator speaks volumes to the way you love her, as a verb. Your mate will realize there are things you cannot do because of time, finances, whatever the circumstances may be. Your mate will understand you cannot cater to their needs all of the time. The point is, when you can do things for them to make their lives better—even a little better---give them the love and support they deserve. Whether it is praying with him/her, cutting grass, rubbing her back, going grocery shopping for her, cooking his favorite meal...whatever the case is...take the necessary steps to show love as a verb whenever possible.

You must make it a point to honor your mate as well. When I consider the three components mentioned in this tenet; this is the one most widely overlooked. Honoring your mate is sometimes tough. You get caught up in the daily routine and the nine to five drama of everyday life. Adding to that, your mate is asking you to do things which may not be easy and they are not necessarily what you want to do. When you think of all of these things, sometimes you forget you are with the person you hold in the highest esteem of anyone in your life. You have to remember this is the person who you claim is most important to you. As you think about doing the things your mate requests of you, honor them in your thoughts as well. Often we forget we are doing something for someone we love and we put our own selfish needs first. Be considerate of their needs and desires above all else. Considering their wants and needs above all others is an important way of honoring your mate. When you talk about your mate to your friends, highlight the things you love and respect about that person. When you introduce your mate to people, introduce them with the title they deserve. Whatever that title is, let others know how important they are to your life. Your mate will appreciate you honoring them in front of others.

Be expressive and happy about who you are with. They have the biggest responsibilities in your lives, they should also be held in the highest esteem. Respect them as they are...the person you decided was worthy of spending your life with, so their decisions are important and crucial to the direction and growth of your marriage. Do not abandon your individuality, but remember they are first and foremost in your life. Praise the good things they do in your life. Give them props for things they may look at as mundane--notice those same mundane things (taking kids to school, picking up dry cleaning, etc.) as important to the nature of your relationship.

Here is another way to honor your mate, specifically for the men. One-hundred percent of the time, your first obligation as a husband or fiancée is to your mate (I know this is for singles, but this was too important to leave out). You have an obligation to your children and to your extended families (each other's children from previous relationships). Remember your wife and children ARE your family. You are all they have. You have to create a sense of security for your wife or future wife. You must be there when no one else is capable of being there. Your wife and children should be your number one priority, as her number one priority should be you. Being the head of the household is more than a person who makes the tough or final decisions, or earns the primary income. You are the person who she looks to for leadership and guidance, but you must also be the person she trusts with her life, and her children's lives. Just as the strongest woman will look to you for guidance, the strongest, wealthiest woman will look to you for security. You can provide security in more ways than making money but earning a living is obviously a component. If she makes the most money, or all of the money, you can make an effort to help her manage it. If you are not yet married and building a relationship, you can help where she wants your assistance to make good decisions on buying or renting a home, major purchases, and all the components of building her life, and filling the gaps where she can use your help. Providing security for your mate is as important as any other way you can honor her. As long as your woman feels secure in you and she trusts you, you will find in her your fiercest supporter and she will recipro-cate the honor for you.

Many will tell you respect is not given, it is earned. Respect has to be mutual to be worthy in a relationship. Both people have to respect one another enough to be honest with the other. Each person has to respect the other to be considerate and caring about one another. You also must respect the roles which both of you decided to play in the relationship. Singles guys, respect the person you are dating as someone who will potentially be your wife. On an even broader scope, keep in mind that if this woman is not destined to be your wife, she is destined to be someone's wife, so treat her with respect and class. I know she is not your wife quite yet, but still respect this woman as a mother, lover, teacher, chef, counselor, arbitrator, disciplinarian, etc., because as you are growing together you will learn these things about her. You will find if you marry her, she will be some, most or all of these things in the context of your marriage. Treat her with high esteem from the time you meet her and she will appreciate it throughout your relationship. Respecting her also extends to respecting her decision making ability, among other things. Men sometimes have a problem trusting a woman's decision making but guys please make yourselves aware women are quite capable of making decisions whether you are around or not, so trust in their ability to do so. Ladies, respect your man as a father, lover, teacher, coach, doctor, arbitrator, spiritual advisor, etc., all the roles he may someday play in your family. A lost art in our contemporary society is the ability to respect your man's ability to give you guidance when you need it. Since we have established he is earning your respect, reciprocate and appreciate him as head of the household and respect his guidance.

This is the ninth tenet because if you have already mastered the other eight tenets and you work at those tenets diligently each day, you are completing the ninth tenet by default. If you are appreciating your mate, you love them openly. If you have chosen not to live together before marriage, you are respecting your mate, your relationship and ultimately, yourself. If you are working on your relationship constantly, as opposed to letting it rest on cruise control, you are honoring your mate and relationship, because they have been put first in your life. There are not many higher honors than to be first in the heart and mind of the person you care about more than anyone else.

I have had several conversations with friends and counterparts about this tenet. The topic has been, "How many people do we know who we can see have these three characteristics in their relationships and both parties in the relationship love, honor and respect one another?" It is astonishing how many couples we know (married or not) who lack at least one of these things from their relationships. I know we all know how to do these things but we have never been taught they are necessary components of building the relationship you want to have. It is so easy to take a relationship for granted and for it to become stagnant quickly. All the tenets work together to make a successful relationship, but if you take this tenet as the beginning and end, it helps to stabilize the entire relationship you build with your mate.

There are some ways these components work together. I have a friend who is married, and he definitely loves, honors and respects his wife. Regardless of the fact, no one and no relationship is one-hundred percent perfect. That being what it is, he can be a little sarcastic at times. As a matter of fact, saying he is a *little* sarcastic is much like saying Albert Einstein was a *little* intelligent. Sometimes his sarcasm will make an issue in his relationship take a more aggressive tone from the beginning of the conversation just because he made an unnecessary comment. His wife knows him and has learned to accept that flaw and loves him anyway. The bigger picture is, he knows his flaws as well and understands the trait does not always come across as loving. He has worked on it, but more importantly, he makes it a point to take the time to work on being loving to his wife. He is always respectful of her and her opinion. Even when he may make an unnecessary sarcastic remark, he still takes the time to listen to everything she has to say. Not just hear what she has to say, but *listen intently* to what she has to say. Having flaws is part of being human. Although they may never completely change, we can make an honest effort to work on improving them. Knowing we have those flaws and still making a conscious effort to be loving, honorable and respectful of our spouse in spite of those flaws is something we have to make a conscious effort to work on.

Finally, as you reflect on this chapter, consider what these traits really mean. Being loving is to have a passionate affection for another person. When you honor someone you revere that person. As you respect someone, you show consideration and a sense of worth for that person. These are very strong characteristics for someone to live up to. Your mate is someone you have an unconditional affection for, you revere them, and you are considerate and have a high sense of worth for them. I reiterate this, because I want to make sure you understand love, honor and respect does not equate to worship. Sometimes, you may feel like your mate is the ultimate and can do no wrong. Ultimately, when it happens they make a mistake which has a huge impact on you, your fall back to reality is much harder than it should have been. You should not put your mate on a pedestal. They are human. They will make mistakes. They have flaws and they are not perfect. I know several people who loved and honored someone to the point where they were borderline worshiping them. Do not worship your mate; worship the Creator. Thank Him for the blessing which is your spouse, fiancée, or significant other. Love your mate. Give them the honor they deserve. Respect them to the highest level. You will be well on your way to a successful relationship.

Chapter Thirteen
LET'S TALK ABOUT…

I am sure some are wondering how I could possibly go this long without touching on this issue. Others are wondering if I am in fact going to touch on it. Still, there are others who feel what they have read so far is helpful, but it is irrelevant until I touch on this topic. Ladies are always looking for answers about it. Guys are looking for ways to get the ladies questions answered, so they can get to it. So many of us think it is the foundation; the building block of a relationship. Some of us think it is inherently problematic and it is not allowed before marriage; and then only to procreate. The truth is everything has its place, and this component of a relationship is no different.

I have passed along my knowledge to you through the nine tenets of a successful relationship. Now, it is up to you how to use them. I gave you the last of the nine tenets in the previous chapter; Love, Honor and Respect Your Mate. Unlike some people's thought processes may assume, those characteristics, are the true building blocks to a relationship. Now it is time to focus on a few things which do not necessarily fall into one tenet or another, but definitely need to be addressed in any book about relationships.

I want to speak to how sex and our expectations around sexual intimacy play a major part in dealing with having a successful relationship. First and foremost, it is a topic that will always need to be addressed by consenting adults. It is going to come up in conversation, and will definitely come up when one partner or the other feels comfortable enough to explore what their limits and boundaries are. Our sexual intimacy is natural. It is the essence of who we are. As people, we are very different in most ways, but when it comes to intimacy, we are more alike than we know. We all have wants and desires. Women who tend to be unsure about how to handle those wants and desires, especially in a new or growing relationship, tend to not want to address those concerns unless put in a position to have to do so. Men, be willing to have those conversations with women, about what they want and need, and what they expect sexually. Alleviating pressures and concerns from early on in a relationship will make the sexual relationship (whenever it starts), be much more comfortable and enjoyable.

Everyone has their thoughts on when to begin a sexual relationship. I have heard anything from, whenever you feel comfortable, to the third date, to ninety days, all the way to marriage. I will speak more about when I think the right time is for a couple to begin a sexual relationship in my next book. I will say that my thoughts on it and His thoughts on it are shared. I know that if both parties are not one-hundred percent comfortable on when to take this journey to intimacy, the party which feels compelled to submit often has a bad experience, because it was not where they really wanted to be. The sex may have been great but the mind must be completely and unequivocally willing for the body to experience the high degree of intimacy which could be shared between the couple.

This may be my favorite topic in the book. I am more than willing to admit it…I love intercourse and I cannot wait until the next time, whenever that is, for me. As a matter of fact, I would not quite go so far to say I am not a nymphomaniac, but those who know me intimately may agree I am a bit "nymphoish." However, I do not take this desire of mine for granted and you should not either. Making love is a beautiful thing and many in our society take it for granted. Our bodies are our temples but when it comes to intimacy we do not treat them as such. So many ladies use sex to get love, and conversely many men use love to get sex. Again, our bodies are temples, and we are distastefully "using" our bodies to get what we want. Love and sex should be a part of the same function. If a woman is giving a man what he wants physically, and he is claiming he loves her to get it (but neither act has much sincerity), is it any wonder the "use" of our bodies is a never ending cycle of disappointment? Ladies, you need to know that sex is never to be used as a bargaining chip for any reason. It devalues the act to the person who is using it as a bargaining chip. I know women now who will say "well, it's only sex." They are right, it is only sex, but it is wired in our DNA to be the way we show affection to the one we love. Remember, one definition of love is passionate affection. A bargaining chip is a long way from being affection, but you have no choice but to share affection through intercourse. It is part of who we are. Once you saturate your mind with an image of what something is supposed to be, you will effectively brainwash yourself to believe that image. Your parents may have taught you that intimacy was to be sacred and only for your husband, but once you started to use it to try to achieve a goal, your perception quickly changed. You basically re-wired yourself to de-value your sexuality.

This is wrong thinking, and it needs to change throughout our society. The problem is perception is reality. Men believe they are not "giving up" anything when they have sex with a woman. Women believe it is a "means" to justify an "end." Both of these trains of thought are incorrect.

A woman who wants the best from a relationship should realize their intimacy is something they own and cannot be taken away. Once a woman begins sleeping with people to get things, attention or love, their intimacy is devalued to themselves. It does not take long before you will start to hope to find love *in spite* of who you have become sexually. Ladies, you can stop this cycle of chasing love with sex, not finding it, feeling used and doing it all over again. If you do not want a sexual relationship, do not have one. Do not allow yourself to be pressured. Start this now…as soon as you close this book! Many women feel like they cannot find another man, because their guy does this or that. You feel as long as you continue satisfying him, even though you are uncomfortable, he will stay with you. This may be true, until he gets tired of the same ole, same ole. Take control of your life, and your individual pursuit of happiness. If you do not want to do it, stop doing it! If he does not want to wait until you are ready, let him go! Trust me on this…he was going to leave eventually anyway! He was not there *for* you; he was never there *for* you. True enough, he was there for one reason or another, but you can be sure it was not because he was willing to fulfill all of your wants and desires; especially the want to not have a sexual relationship until you were completely comfortable with it. The most amazing thing about this line of thinking is, if you want specific qualities in someone and you wait for them, when you find them, the wait is even more rewarding than you ever dreamed of.

Even I have been guilty of trying to convince someone to fulfill my selfish desires. True enough, we had already went there before but here is what I understand now and what men and women should always understand: When the other person is not ready, maybe you can convince them to take it there—but you are convincing the heart (the heart is deceitful) and not the mind, so it will not be what you expect or deserve and your relationship may never be the same.

Fellas, fellas, fellas…we have our own set of issues. One of those is rarely addressed, but I mentioned it earlier. You feel like when you have sex with a woman, you are not really "giving up" anything. I will touch on it more but you need to learn you are giving of yourself, your spirit, and the essence of who you are when you are intimate with a woman. Guys still want to believe we should have a caveman mentality. Hit the "food" in the head, bring it back to the cave, have the woman cook it, then later that evening do whatever she will allow, wake up in the morning and run it all over again. Contrary to popular opinion, guys, you are not equivalent to a dog that can sense a female dog in heat and you are running around with the little pink thing hanging out. We are so much more than that. First and foremost, we have a "sexual imprint," much like a woman does. As a society, we follow our expectations; what you have seen in your environment as you matured, and what is acceptable on television, movies, the internet and other media. You have a societal expectation of your sexuality, just as a woman does. Society and the environment you live in create that imprint. I see many of our expectations are misguided, because our thought processes have been transformed for the worse, due to several factors (many of which I will touch on in my follow up book). Guys need to support one another in being faithful to one woman, as opposed to supporting each other in trying to see how many trophies they can attain. Just from this thinking alone (trophy hunting), we start off with a devalued sexuality from a young age, because we do not realize our sexual imprint is also affected from this methodology of thinking.

Next, we take these misguided methods of thinking into serious relationships. How can we really find out about someone in-depth when we are actually more focused on how we can get up on the girl who sits a few offices down from us at work? If we learn to devote the time and attention we use on creating the bad habit of chasing more than one woman at a time into using the tenets in this book to build a solid relationship, we will have immensely stronger, more meaningful relationships. I know some guys who have been so terribly re-wired, it is as if they think they are *supposed* to cheat. It is so bad, it is to the point where you would think they read, "Cheat on your mate" as one of the Ten Commandments. It's a sad footnote to our current society.

It is true that men have developed a more innate ability to "take it or leave it." We tend to be able to be able to detach affection from sex much more easily than women. The problem there is when we start detaching affection from our sexual nature, there is not much left to our sexual nature. We become very empty and shallow as sexual people. I am a romantic. You can hate on me if you like, but my woman will know I love her if I am indeed in love, because I will romance her as much as I can. I want to be intimate on a different level. I want to experience her touch…not just sexually, but spiritually. I want to experience her smell to the point where when she enters a room, I know it is her without seeing her. I want to experience all of the essence of who she is. If I could detach affection from sex, I could screw everything moving, and miss out on who a woman really is. Do not get it wrong, sex is fun, but it can be fun with one partner. I once heard Roger Staubach say, "I enjoy sex as much as Joe Namath, I just enjoy it with one woman, my wife." Those are the kinds of messages I would like to see still permeate in our society. What I want guys to understand is when you are physically intimate with a woman; you are giving of yourself spiritually, and emotionally as well as physically. Have you ever thought about how one woman makes you feel a certain way which no other woman could get out of you? Now, if you are not in tune with how to treat that woman, and how to experience that woman's intimacy, you may miss out on the blessing you were meant to receive. You could go around the rest of your life, having sex with anyone and everyone; ultimately feeling empty about all of it. All of this could happen because you could not experience the same intimacy with the others that you experienced with this one woman but you could not stop chasing other women.

When one of my relationships ended, a young lady told me she learned something from our relationship. She said she did not know before we were together that men could be so loving, caring and affectionate. She did not see it in her family growing up, and she did not see it in her previous relationships. One of the beautiful things about life is the fact we can choose to learn each and every day. She could have chosen to simply see the end of the relationship, and not get anything from it, other than it is over and that is it. This woman took the time to reflect and learn from our situation, and I hope she takes that knowledge into her future relationships. You never know how you are touching someone's life when you become a part of their lives. Guys, we can be leaders in so many ways. Be a leader in showing an appropriate amount of intimacy in your relationship. Lead by talking about sex from the early stages of the relationship. Show maturity in your sexual imprint by not treating adultery as though it is a game, and you want to see how long you can play until you get caught. Ladies, learn that sex is not made to acquire love; it is a component of love. Never find yourself willing to try to trade one for another. When the right mate comes along and you have communicated your needs and desires to one another, you should now have a better idea how to approach intimacy in the context of a successful relationship.

Chapter Fourteen
BABE, I WOULD LOVE TO BUT...

adies, I am sure you have heard this plenty of times. I am guessing you have probably heard that phrase or something similar much too often. "Babe, I would love to take you on a vacation but we can't afford it right now." "Babe, I would love to take you shopping but we can't do it right now." First of all, money is not a root or building block of a relationship. That is why there is not a tenet speaking exclusively to finances in this book. You can have a more happiness in a relationship where the couple makes thirty-five thousand a year as opposed to a couple who makes one hundred thousand annually. Be clear on that ladies (and guys); your happiness in your relationship should not be based in money. Referring to a phrase from a previous chapter, a relationship based on someone's financial situation is totally an association of convenience. Be that as it may, finances are a key component to any relationship. Guys, we have to be able to direct the steps of the relationship financially. That means, whether you make the most money or not, you need to be able to guide how the money is being spent and saved for you as a couple to get to where you want to go in life together financially. We have to create less of those catch phrases, "Darling, I wish we could do that but…" If you want to keep your woman happy, you develop ways to make the things happen that she wants to happen, within reason. Planning ahead is a great way to do this. Often, when ladies get to do what they want to do, whether it is go shopping in New York, or to a ski trip in the Smokies, the fact that you have planned and made it happen makes her look forward to the moment and appreciate it even more. The amount of what you are spending is not relevant. The fact you take the time and effort to do what she wants is what matters. It may be as little as eating at a very nice restaurant once in a while. Prepare for it, make it happen, and she will love you for it.

Now I am sure there are a couple of people out there who I have dated in the past who may be trippin' that I have the "nerve" to write a chapter like this one. I am the first to admit, I have had problems managing my finances in a couple of my past relationships. I was smart enough to learn and grow from those mistakes and do a better job going forward. Regardless, I am sure I am still getting hated on for my "learning experiences." The reason I think I am probably being hated on is women do not let that go so easily. Learn from my experience, guys. Take care of your business financially in your relationships. It is a part of the characteristic of providing the security women need. During one of my experiences, I was living with someone (first mistake). It was her house (second mistake). We never had a conversation on what she expected me to do financially in specific terms. We would have little conversations and comments here and there, but it was never "you pay for this, I'll pay for that." We had a total breakdown in communication (third mistake). Therefore, you combine those mistakes with the fact I was mismanaging my money (fourth, and she might say biggest mistake), and I was not doing what I needed to do financially within this relationship. Needless to say, it did not work out. Another thing I did wrong was while my heart was always in the right place, but my bank account did not always line up with my heart. I love to travel and she did as well. I would go on trips or whatever she wanted to do. The problem was not the fact I did not have the money to do it but the fact I did not plan for it financially and on one or two occasions it was a financial strain.

The takeaway I want you to get from my example is that I although I had the money to do whatever I wanted to do, I did not manage what I had very well. It does not matter if you make ten dollars per hour or one hundred fifty thousand per year; if you do not manage it well, the money will be detrimental to your relationship. When you work together and talk about what you want to do and what you want to accomplish together with your money, plan ahead. Follow your budget as closely as you can, and prepare for the opportunity to have some fun or just some good quality time together.

I have another friend; I will refer to her as Alicia. Alicia has a man who loves her very much. He manages his money just fine. The problem is he does not make any money. "Not any money" may be an overstatement but not by much. He makes very little money. She cannot spend quality time with him, she cannot see him, she cannot do much of anything with him because he simply does not have any cheese to make it happen. It is ok to not have a lot of money. It is not ok to not have *any* money. I am someone who understands that everything has its time, and your time to get compensated for what you are working toward in life sometimes takes time. That is fine but do not use that as an excuse or crutch. Romance does require some financing…just as everything in life does. If you are waiting to get that acting break, or publishing deal; that is fine, but you need to be waiting tables, working in a call center or creating some form of income if you plan on having a relationship.

If you are in a relationship and you have no money; you must do something (legally of course) to get some income flowing. Ambition may make her horny, but it does not pay to get her mani/pedi. If you are having problems managing your money, look for outlets to help you develop a budget and have the discipline to stick to it. Some decisions you have to make will be tough decisions but some sacrifice now may position you for a stronger life together later. Make sure your woman is a part of all of the financial conversations, and how you (plural-as a couple) manage the money you have. She will appreciate being respected to be a part of those conversations and you both will realize it is a part of the journey together. Learn to enjoy managing your money. As long as you control the money and the money does not control you; you will be fine.

I have been man-bashing up to this point in this chapter but ladies can be challenged on this topic as well. Some of you like to shop and I am not one to hate on you about that. I do think sometimes you should do things in moderation. For example, I know women who will not reschedule a hair appointment but then have to deal with not being able to pay a utility. I realize how important it is for women to look great, as a matter of fact I totally agree. Maybe you should buy the new "magic flat iron" on the infomercial to prepare for the rare days like this which sometimes may happen. I also understand that just as men are capable of mismanaging money, women sometimes have the challenge of prioritizing as well. If you are considering buying an accessory to match an outfit as opposed to paying a bill…you are having a conversation you should not be having to begin with. The same methodology I gave to the men applies to the ladies. Plan ahead, and prioritize. When you think "why put off for tomorrow what I can buy on credit today" then the day the credit card bill is due you are trying to decide whether to pay the bill or get the purse that matches the outfit you bought on the credit card, there is a problem. I am not generalizing. I know all women are not shop-aholics just as all men do not mismanage money. What I am saying is no matter what the situation is ladies, you must also be considerate of your mate and what he is bringing to the table financially. If you wish he was "ballin" but he is not, then do not try to spend his money like it is magically reappearing in his bank account as soon as you swipe his card. I have a friend who knows a lady who has a "fetish" for travelling to shop. She is in her thirties with no husband or children. At least once a month she takes a trip to go shopping or hang out in a nice spot. New York, L.A., Vegas…wherever there is good shopping, she is going. That is great, I think she should do her thing since she is single and not in a relationship. Her challenge is she has gotten very accustomed to this lifestyle. Now when she talked to my friend about expectations of a relationship, she was talking about how she likes to travel, and the fact she wants to shop in many cities and see a lot of different places. My friend is a realist. He felt like he could not support that lifestyle, so they never entered into a relationship. The point of the example is to understand when you enter a relationship you have to make concessions, sometimes financial, as opposed to what you were doing when you were single. Even as boyfriend/girlfriend you now have a commitment to spend quality time together, get to know one another, and build your relationship so you find out if you are indeed compatible for taking more steps in the future. That being the case, you cannot live like you are single anymore. If you are living like you are single, then you are indeed single mentally and you are passing time in your relationship as opposed to building something lasting and successful.

I think the most important component of dealing with finances in a relationship is to take care of the finances together. The economy is always changing. People change jobs, change spending habits, change areas of the country which changes costs of living. There are so many variables to finances. The key is to work through the challenges and issues together. Be open and honest about your financial situation to one another. Being upfront about your individual financial situation is another component of the trust and security you develop in truly successful relationships. Many times the relationship is strengthened when financial times are the toughest. When you learn to look to one another for support, the almighty dollar does not seem so mighty anymore. There are some women I have dated which I could have spent time with in a *cave*, and had nothing. I would have been happy simply because they graced me with their presence. I would be cool just holding that person to keep them from being scared of the bats in the cave. I know that is an over-the-top analogy but it is true. I am quite sure it is an over-used phrase, but this is so very true: It is not what you have, but it is how you use what you have. When you learn to manage your finances in a positive, effective way; you will help to create success in your relationship.

Chapter Fifteen

FROM THIS DAY FORWARD

You have so many things to think about as you build and cultivate your relationship. I have talked about quite a few over the course of this book. There is a topic rarely discussed in this context but we need to think about this and be more aware of it, since our culture has a significant amount of single parents. When you bring two people together with a different set of morals, values and upbringings, it is tough and can be very difficult. If you can get past all the things I have discussed as far as things you have to do to make your relationship successful, there are still other variables a lot of us never have considered. This is a chapter for those who have to take into consideration more than just themselves and their significant other when they think about starting a family.

I have a friend who shared this with me. She told me about a nephew she has, who is not biologically her nephew. Although that is the case, it does not matter to her in the least if he is biologically her nephew or not. As far as she is concerned, he is her nephew, period, bottom line! There is someone in her family who did not mean any harm, but once said something to the extent that the little boy's mom needed to "take care of her son" making it abundantly clear that the boy was "her son" and not their blood. My friend has the utmost respect for her family. She was gracious in reminding the family member that the child was as much a part of the family as any child in the bloodline. As gracious as she was to that family member, you would not have known it when she talked to me about it because she snapped! She let me know that family member was wrong and this child was as much "theirs" as anyone's! The passion which she spoke about this little man on that day gave me a respect for her to another level which I do not think she even realizes to this point. She was defending a child who had some challenges but whom she could not have loved with more fervor and passion than if she was his mother! We can all learn from this story.

The child's challenges were not the point. The bloodline was not the point. The point is that when the child became a part of their family by marriage, he became wholeheartedly, unconditionally and undoubtedly a part of their family. She loves him as if he were not just a part of her bloodline, but her own child. When we bring families together with children from past relationships; we have to be conscious of this. I have heard women say this—"When you marry me, you marry my children. We are a package deal." The fact that a single parent and their children are a package deal is an understatement. If you become a part of a relationship with someone with children, whether the parent is a man or woman, you have accepted the responsibility to rear those children just as a parent would.

There are so many different situations out there with people who bring children into relationships. Each one is different, each with its own dynamic and each one has a set of rules and standards a new parent has to adjust to. There are situations where a new parent has to adjust to seeing their new child every other weekend, or sending them away every other weekend. There are about as many variations on visitations rights as there are days in the year, so I will not elaborate, but I will mention this: One of the first things a new parent must do is be supportive. Be supportive of whatever arrangements are worked out and be a conduit for success in these situations. Often, these are sensitive situations. There can be a lot of hurtful feelings including, but not limited to pride, anger, bitterness, rage, contempt, spite...and for some of the women I know, those are the good qualities. Before you bite my head off ladies, I know somewhere right now, there is some lady calling some dude "trifling" so buy a latte and keep reading. My point is, when there is someone new to a situation, take the time to adjust and feel your way through it. There is a great chance someone is not going to like you. Try not to take it personally. Simply put, they do not really have some irrelevant distaste for you, they just do not like the situation and you are one more component of it. There are a lot of different dynamics out there, and women and men have to be understanding to the dynamic of a relationship with children from a previous relationship.

There are a couple of derivative things I want to touch on as far as the dynamic of a parent/child relationship. Notice I did not say stepchild. I cannot tell you what is right or wrong as far as what your child should call you or what you should call your child. Those are family decisions and they are made on a case-by-case basis. I cannot tell you one thing or another is one-hundred percent correct. I can tell you this: you must treat a stepchild like a child of your own. They must respect you and you must respect them. I know there will be certain boundaries set for step-parents in some cases, and some families situations may present certain "lines" a step-parent should not cross. Again, those are case by case issues and there is no set-in-stone, all-encompassing solution. I can tell you whatever level of respect that is expected in your home must be extended to any step-children. You cannot have two kids in the same age range, with one child who can come in and out at whatever time because his biological parent may think he does not need a curfew, and another child who has a 9:30 curfew, but if you had your choice they would be on the same schedule. Your children (kids, step-kids, exchange students, cats, dogs---anyone living "utility-bill challenged") must have a consistent message for everyone to be on the same page and for everyone to respect you and your home as it should be. Not only could extending boundaries make the parent-child relationship tougher, but one sibling may feel slighted if another gets "special" treatment simply because their parent is not happy. For example, in my case, I have the philosophy: "As for me and my house, we will serve the Lord." I ain't trippin' if you do not want to learn to serve Him but you will not be living in my house. My friend loved her nephew although they were related by marriage. You must love every child as much as your own children. That is tough for any parent to hear, I think especially some mothers. It is not selfish to feel that way, so do not think that way about yourself.

You did carry this child for nine months. You had to look at his/her Dad even when you would have rather watched grass grow or paint dry (you ladies who have been hormonal--you feel me). You had to get up with them in the middle of the night and change them and feed them. I did these things too, so I am with you. I just did not have to have an epidural (thanks to all that is good in Heaven and on Earth!). You had to clean noses, stay home from work because the kids are sick, and listen to "back talk" when they could not even make complete sentences. I cherish all the mothers in the world for that. Without you, there would be no "us," and I thank you for that. That being said, if you make the decision to marry someone with a little selfish, funky-attitude, spoiled brat of a six-year-old, you have to love them as you would love your own child. Love is endless…you can give as much as you want and you have an endless supply. Supply this child who is coming into your life with the love and caring you would provide for your own child. Developing a bond with another child does not break or tarnish the bond you have with your own child…it only strengthens it. Even when children may not get along at first; later in life they love and rely on their siblings, whether they are bloodline siblings or not. Our siblings hold a special place in our hearts. Having more just gives children more room to grow, love and appreciate someone else who is truly special in their heart.

I talked about Moms and entering into relationships with children so now let me speak on the Dads for a moment. I am a father myself, and I have dated a few women with children. I want to talk about a couple of those situations. I must say I have always been blessed with the ability to become close to and love the children but in some instances, even my judgment has be clouded. Something to think about as you read these stories: It is not how you think of yourself in certain situations but how you allow yourself to be perceived. No matter what reality may be, if the perception is not what it needs to be, the reality is irrelevant because to the person who matters (your significant other), you are not doing enough. Case and point:

We'll call this young lady Stephanie. Stephanie and I dated for a while, and she had two beautiful children. One of the children is quite a bit older than the other. After spending some time together, I became pretty close to the children. The younger child's father was involved in his child's life, while the older child's father was not. Stephanie noticed I would go out of my way to do things for the older child, and not the younger child. I do not think she believed I did not care for the younger child, but her perception (without her having the benefit of seeing my subconscious thoughts) was that I was simply "favoring" one over the other. She could not be sure of the reason but she brought it up one night. We discussed and argued this point at length. I could not convince her I was not "favoring" one over the other. Looking back, I might have subconsciously done more for one than the other, but I loved them both equally. The difference was, the younger one had a father being a part of his life, the father was not around for the older one and it was easy to see that was something he was missing in his life. He did not want or need for anything material, but he also did not have a father to talk to and do "father/son" things with. Stephanie's perception is that I was playing favorites, when in my heart of hearts I was not doing that. What I did not know then which I totally understand now is that it does not matter if I was or not. She was my significant other at the time, and I needed to change her perception. If I cannot change it, I will always fight this battle with her because what she sees is her reality. I believe I did a better job at it as time moved along. As a footnote to this example: We single parents do a great job at what we do. The truth is we can be the best parent we can be but we can never replace the other parent. She could not replace his Dad. For that matter, I could not either, but I felt like I could fill a little of the void this child was missing in his life.

That situation was a great learning experience for me. If she and I would have gotten married, I would have had to step up my game and accept the responsibilities as a parent for both kids to the fullest; not just one. I could have done that and not stepped on any toes. It just took a little love and caring from me to the children and the ability to work with my significant other and developing my place in their lives.

I have another example of how perception is reality until everyone gets on the same page. The woman I spoke of earlier that I had the two part relationship with had a child. He and I were very close; I loved him to no end and I still do to this day. I have not seen him in years and if he ever calls me and needs anything and I can provide it for him, it is his, sight unseen. The challenge in this situation is my significant other at the time once gave me a very in-depth lecture about how I was not close to her child. She compared his relationship to me with other father/son relationships in her family. That is a mistake. Obviously, you have to have some reference points, but look at each relationship based on its own merits. I loved little man to death, but I know she could not see it how she wanted to see it and that is my fault. He and I were not very affectionate; really in a lot of ways just "cool." What she could not see was he and I were both extremely nonchalant about everything. You have to do quite a bit to evoke sincere emotion from either of us. Since she never saw what she thought was "a bond," she felt like I was not as close to him as I should have been. We bonded in different ways. I can remember one time he was really upset with someone, and the fact that I had his back meant so much to him. He and I talked about it later, he gave me a high five, and that was that. No intense emotional moment…just a quick high-five; he went and watched cartoons, and I was wishing the Cowboys were playing (it was right before football season). I never told his mom about this and he was so little, he may not even remember it. The point is, it drew us closer, but her perception did not change because she could not see the bonding. I was wrong in not showing her where I was in her son's life, and how important he was to me. Like most of you ladies, she may have been right most of the time but this time she was wrong. She should have allowed us to bond in our own way. I cannot, beyond the shadow of a doubt, tell everyone how to raise their children. I can advise you to treat all the children with similar age ranges in the house with the same rules for everyone. Everyone is an individual and there will be adjustments here and there. The central theme is if you treat your children with love, respect, care, teach humility, instill discipline, treat them as you would want to be treated and pray for them all; merging families can be a lot easier than we make it out to be.

Chapter Sixteen
IT IS UP TO YOU

We have reached the end of our journey…or shall I say, we have reached the end of our journey in this book. This is only the beginning. Now it is up to you to take these solid, proven theories and place them into application. The great thing about this journey is, when you apply these techniques, your life's journey (much like the journey through the book) is very simple. We hear people talk everyday about the fact they do not want drama. Well, the fact is, there will always be some drama in our lives. There will be a hurdle to overcome. I am sure there will be obstacles where you expect smooth sailing. Trials and tribulations are promised in this life. Within life and the context of any relationship, it is truly not what you are faced with but how you deal with the obstacle you are faced with.

I have yet to share a beautiful component about these tenets. It is like a basketball player who has been playing for years and one day he finds his sweet spot. He is still an average shooter from everywhere else on the court, but now, as if by magic, when he gets to his favorite spot on the court, he is automatic. This component is like when you have worked at mastering a difficult course you are taking in school. You work and work…the journey seems long and rough. When you finally understand that subject and you have it mastered, the feeling of euphoria (as well as relief) is amazing. Not only have you conquered something you not-so-long ago sucked at, but now you are the master of its domain. Fellas, do not get it twisted…this does not mean to start trying to master your woman. Then I may have to write a follow up on how to sleep snake-style (with your eyes open). When I say this component makes you feel like you have mastered something, it makes you feel like you have mastered building a good relationship which is actually giving something back to you. You now control your relationship! You know how to get what you want out of your relationship! I am not saying manipulate-just the opposite. I am saying you have built a trustworthy, successful relationship built on doing the things you need to do to keep your mate happy and energized about being with you. Now that you do them, before you even start to notice, your mate will be working to do the things you like as well. This is the secret to seeing results in thirty days. It takes about twenty-one days to create a habit, so by thirty days it should become a way of life. After you have put your energy into one of these tenets for a month, you will see your partner reciprocate (if they do not already) your efforts. At first, they may think you are guilty of something. That is great; at least you know they are paying attention to your behavior. Stick with what you are doing. Keep giving them appreciation, or start dating them again if you have not been doing so. Whichever tenet you want to start with; go for it! Get the ball rolling, and in thirty days, look for that improvement. Start a second tenet and add it to the first one for the next thirty days. Re-energize and strengthen your relationships through these components. If you already have some of these things down, great, no need to change that component. When you are ready to add a new one, incorporate the new thought process into your way of thinking and make a concerted effort to follow it. I think most diets would work, but since none of us follow them for over thirty days (if that long), who really knows? You have to stay with it. If you stay with it, these tenets will change your life and the life of your mate.

I used a lot of great experiences which I was either a part of or had the privilege to have someone share with me. There are people who thought my advice and thinking processes were worth sharing with you and I am grateful to them for that. Obviously, I chose to use aliases to protect the guilty (and the innocent). Some people will know I used their stories, some probably will not. The most important thing is, I hope they learned from these tenets just as you have. I love each and every person who was a part of a story, or whose story I shared as an example. I would never put anyone on blast (other than myself), so unless they choose to share, no one will ever be able to put a name or face with a story. I wanted to say this in the book, because I want everyone to know how much I love and appreciate my friends and everyone associated in any way with this book.

In life, some people will disagree with you. Some people will not find anything you say amusing. Others will not find you attractive. You cannot be all things to all people. I say this to let you know, I know there will be detractors with this book. My tenets will work, no matter race, gender, nationality, etc., whatever the demographics of your relationship; these nine tenets are solid foundational components of a successful relationship. That being said, everyone is entitled to an opinion. I do not expect everyone to agree with each and every component of this book. For those who fit that category, I will challenge you to this: If you disagree with my thoughts on living together; not a problem—try appreciating more. If you disagree with my thoughts on working on your relationship; not a problem—try loving, honoring, and respecting more. My point is, find something that works for you, as opposed to trying to convince yourself or someone else why something does not work. Do you own "case study" and watch exactly how much it changes lives to appreciate or keep hanging out with (dating) your significant other. I would be remiss if I did not show a little extra appreciation for one person in particular, the person who I had the two-part relationship with. I spoke about a lot of people in different scenarios, but that specific relationship was touched on in several chapters. I learned a lot from that relationship. I grew so much. More than anything else, I learned that love is a verb. I also realize we cannot go back and change anything. What we go through makes us who we are today. I used to think it would be cool to go back and change things but if you change one thing, you have to change everything after that moment in time. I am very thankful and blessed to be who I am and where I am with my life, so I do not want to change a thing. Have the same perspective about your relationships. Move forward and grow in your current and future relationships. I do not regret anything about any of these relationships I describe where I "put myself on blast" and I would not change anything that happened during or since. I hope you feel the same about your relationships. Grow and learn from them. No point on dwelling in the past, but use the past to learn from and not to repeat the same mistakes over and over. My boo taught me about love and I taught her that a man could show he is loving. Ladies, I want you to learn that as well. When it comes to romance, men can be "romantically challenged," but remember we can be loving as well. Guys, make sure you understand what love is, its intricacies, its substance, its essence and how to approach love in your own unique situation. As I pass along my appreciation to my friend, I would like to say, "Dominique," I wish you happiness and may God bless you and your family.

As I come to a close, I want you to know I have enjoyed teaching and learning about relationships and I hope you have as well. I hope you consider these tenets as steps in the right direction toward growth of a long-lasting, loving relationship. I have given the building blocks of a successful relationship, now it is up to you to apply those components. I will share with you in the future the "Tenth tenet." It will be an in-depth look at the glue that holds the nine tenets together. Until that time, my prayer for you is that every relationship you have be one that you learn from. May every relationship you enter be one you are able to teach something to someone. Finally, my wish is the most successful relationship you ever encounter is one the Creator has divinely blessed to be a relationship which lasts a lifetime.

www.ingramcontent.com/pod-product-compliance
Lightning Source LLC
Chambersburg PA
CBHW051455250726

48655CB00001B/419